Deliver Us from Evil

Reading the Psalms as Poetry

Alexander Ryrie

DARTON·LONGMAN+TODD

First published in 2004 by
Darton, Longman and Todd Ltd
1 Spencer Court
140–142 Wandsworth High Street
London
SW18 4JJ

ISBN 0 232 52538 2

A catalogue record for this book is available from the British Library.

Designed by Sandie Boccacci
Phototypeset in 10/12.5pt Times New Roman
by Intype Libra Ltd
Printed and bound in Great Britain by Page Bros, Norwich, Norfolk

Contents

Preface

The Psalms of the Old Testament are read and used in many different ways by different people. This book is intended mainly for the general reader who is prepared to take a serious and thoughtful interest in them. Unfortunately there has for long been something of a division between the way the Psalms are read and understood by academic scholars, and the use that is made of them for liturgical and devotional purposes. I believe, however, that the growing scholarly interest in a literary approach to the Bible makes it more possible to engage with the Psalms in a way which is both scholarly and devotional, and which is accessible to the non-specialist reader.

Much of the book is centred on the theme of deliverance from evil, a theme which I believe is central to the Psalms. This is a very large topic about which a great deal more could be said. I have chosen not to venture forth on a more general discussion of such a wide and difficult subject, which could take me well beyond my competence, but to limit my study to the Psalms. I hope, however, that some readers may care to reflect on the wider implications of the psalmists' thoughts and images, not least for the Christian understanding of the atonement.

Quotations from the Bible are taken from the New Revised Standard Version (NRSV) unless otherwise stated. Psalm verses are numbered according to the English versions, not the Hebrew text. In order to respect Jewish principles, I have not used the vocalised form of the *tetragrammaton*, the divine name YHWH. Even when the vocalised form is used by writers from whom I quote I have taken the liberty of altering this to 'Yhwh'.

Although I am not unaware of gender issues, I have continued to use the masculine pronoun with respect to God. This is partly because this is, of course, the usage of the Psalms which I am studying; and partly because I have found no sensible, readily usable and theologically acceptable alternative to a gendered pronoun. I also refer to the authors of the psalms as 'he'. This is largely because I feel sure that the psalms will have been written mainly by men, but partly also to avoid the clumsy circumlocution of constantly repeating 'he or she'.

My warm thanks are due to John Armson who read and commented on an earlier draft of the book, and gave me much encouragement; and to my wife Isabel for help with putting the text into appropriate computerised form, and for her constant support.

ACR

Chapter 1

Poems and Prayers

The Psalms of the Old Testament have been a spiritual resource for people of different religious traditions for thousands of years. During this time methods of interpreting them have kept changing, and they have been understood in a great many ways. My aim in this book is to present one particular way of reading and interpreting the Psalms, based on their special character as poems addressed to God, and more especially on some of the poetic images, or word pictures, which we find in them. At the same time I will use this approach to explore one particular theme that runs through the Psalter, that of how God delivers from evil and distress. I believe that this theme is central to the Book of Psalms, and that even when it is not immediately apparent it is never far below the surface. I hope that such an approach will both assist a devotional reading of individual psalms, and also provide an insight into the meaning of the Psalms as a whole.

The Psalter, or Book of Psalms, is a collection of poems, most of which are prayers. The very large majority of the 150 psalms are addressed, in whole or in part, to God. Although the title of the book in the Hebrew Bible (*Tehillim*) means 'Praises', there is good reason to believe that in early times both Jews and Christians referred to the Psalms as 'Prayers' (*Tephilloth*).[1] These prayers, however, are also poems, written in Hebrew poetic verse form. These two features of the Psalms – their poetic quality and their character as prayers addressed to God – provide the basis for this exploration. A few words should, therefore, be said at the start about each of them.

The Psalms as Poetry

Although it has always been known that the Psalms were written in poetic

form, their special character as poetry has in the past often been overlooked. They have been read, and sometimes printed in translation, as if
they were simply prose. In recent years, however, there has been a growing interest in the Psalms as poetry.[2] It is increasingly recognised that to
read the Psalms in this way is not to reduce them to 'mere literature', and
to deny their truth content or religious value. On the contrary, seeing them
as poetry enables us to understand them in a fresh way and to find in them
new, and perhaps deeper forms of truth. The psalmists, it has been said,
were 'authentic theologians', who expressed their faith through poetic
idiom.[3] As another recent writer has put it: 'To know the psalms are poetic
is not to forget that they are Scripture. To read and hear them as Scripture
requires that one receive them also as poetry.'[4] It is important to recognise
that alongside the truths of a more logical and rational kind that may be
found in the Psalms, there is a poetic or aesthetic truth which is of equal
theological and spiritual importance. This is true in a sense of all poetry.
The modern poet Cecil Day Lewis speaks of a poetic truth which 'is not,
like scientific truth, verifiable', but which operates upon us to bring about
a 'furtherance of life'. 'The truth', he says, 'is in the passion.'[5]

The expression of truth in this fashion has continued to be part of the
eastern, Semitic tradition. We find it, for example, much later in the great
Syrian Christian theologian Ephrem, who wrote much of his theology in
poetry. For such writers poetry expresses a different kind of truth, which
is something experienced, something inner, which may be inexpressible in
logical, rational form, and which may be paradoxical.[6] This applies also to
much of the Old Testament, which is part of that same tradition, and in
particular to the Psalter. 'The Psalms', says Kraus, 'are artistic poems,
whose form cannot be ignored in order to abstract a few bundles of teach-
ings for a theology of the Psalms', because beauty is 'one specific way of
expressing truth'.[7]

What is it, then, that defines Hebrew poetry, that distinguishes the
Psalms and other 'poetic' books from the prose sections of the Bible? To
some extent it is the use of certain formal or stylistic devices. Many
commentators have described what are often called the 'forms of Hebrew
poetry'; features of Hebrew form and style which are thought to characterise its poetry. One of these is said to be 'metre'. In earlier times it was
believed that underlying the language of the Psalms there were Hebrew
metrical forms similar to those of classical Greek and Latin poetry, based
on the number of syllables in a line of verse. More recently scholars have
taken a different view of Hebrew metre, arguing that it was based, not on
the number of syllables, but on the number of stresses, or stressed

syllables, in a line.[8] But none of these attempts to identify a metrical system can be said to have been wholly successful. For while many psalms can be shown to have a regular arrangement of stressed syllables, there are many others which can only be made to conform to a fixed metre by resorting to considerable emendation of the text *metri causa* (as it is put), by altering the text to make it fit the supposed metre. Apparently metre, if it exists at all, cannot be regarded as an essential feature of Hebrew poetry.[9]

There are, however, other stylistic devices which can be clearly seen in Hebrew verse, such as assonance, alliteration and *chiasmus*; and above all parallelism – the convention by which a line of verse is made up of two (or sometimes three) clauses or components which are parallel to one another both in form and sense, with the second (and third) repeating, developing or enhancing the thought of the first in different words. Parallelism has long been recognised as an important feature of Hebrew poetry, and recent studies have demonstrated more clearly just what a subtle, flexible and sensitive form of expression it is.[10] Its use in a variety of subtle ways adds to both the aesthetic quality and the depth of meaning of Hebrew poetry. Nevertheless, it can be shown that most of these stylistic devices, including parallelism, are to be found not only in poetry but also, to a greater or lesser degree, in parts of the Hebrew Bible which are usually designated as prose. There appears to be what Miller (following Kugel) has called a 'poetry-prose continuum'.[11] Although stylistic devices occur more frequently at the poetry end of the continuum, many prose passages in the Old Testament, especially in the prophets, are written in a 'high rhetorical style' that has many features in common with the poetry of the Psalms and other poetic books.[12] Thus it is clear that these stylistic devices alone do not create poetry.

Is there then nothing essential which distinguishes the Psalms as poetry?[13] It is important to remember that poetry is not simply a matter of form. To qualify as poetry a piece of writing must possess not only formal features but also certain qualities which it is less easy to define. In genuine poetry stylistic devices are allied to, and used in the service of, these less tangible qualities. These include, in the case of religious poetry in particular, what is sometimes called *loftiness of thought*, the expression of thoughts and sentiments which are not trivial, ordinary, mundane or banal, but serious, imaginative, potentially inspiring, and above the level of our common thoughts. Along with this there goes *intensity of emotion* or feeling, the use and arrangement of words in such a way as to arouse and provide a vehicle for powerful feelings of different kinds. Both these qualities are found in large measure in the Psalms.

But alongside these broad and basic qualities, there are two other distinctive characteristics of poetry in general, and Hebrew poetry in particular, which are important for the interpretation of the Psalms. One is a certain *ambiguity of meaning* which leaves words or phrases open to different interpretations.[14] In Hebrew this is achieved in part by a 'terseness of style',[15] a clipped and compact way of writing in which things are stated very briefly and sometimes enigmatically (often by the device of omitting words or forms such as the definite article or the 'accusative particle', which would be expected in prose); and in part by other stylistic devices (such as a flexible movement between the 'perfect' and 'imperfect' forms of verbs[16]). In these ways the psalmists provide hints of various shades of meaning, and leave scope for readers or users of the psalm to exercise their own imagination in interpreting it, as we shall attempt to do.

The other significant characteristic of the poetry of the Psalms is its use of *imagery*. The Psalms are particularly rich in poetic imagery, especially tropes in the form of metaphors and similes, some of which have too often been understood in an excessively prosaic and literal fashion. Imagery is not simply a stylistic device, but a means not only of enhancing the aesthetic quality but also of pointing to deeper truths than can be stated in non-figurative language, as we shall see in greater detail in Chapter 3. There is, therefore, as P. D. Miller has recently said, a 'need for a focus once again on the figures as a major aspect of poetic style'.[17]

Viewing the Psalms as poetic texts can thus involve various things. It can mean paying attention to their internal structure and to formal matters such as the style and artistic conventions which the psalmists used. It can mean opening ourselves to their poetic beauty, and letting ourselves *feel* it at a deep level. But one important way of grasping some of the poetic truth of the Psalms is to pay attention to their use of imagery. By doing this we may open windows into the meaning of the Psalms; and for our purposes this may reveal something of the psalmists' understanding of evil and deliverance.

Addressing God

As has been said, the very large majority of the psalms are addressed, in whole or in part, to God.[18] In some cases this applies only to one or two verses, but in many others the whole psalm is couched in the second person, spoken directly to God. Moreover, the majority of those which do not address God directly include an invitation to approach God or to praise him; and almost all refer in one way or another to aspects of a direct relationship between people and God. It is not too much to say that the psalms, even those which do not address God directly, are poems which are to be spoken or sung in the presence of God, as part of the people's approach to him. What is more, many psalms move quickly and easily between speaking directly to God and speaking about him. One verse addresses God in the second person and the next refers to him in the third (for example, 23:3–4; 30:3–4; 57:1–2), in a way which can disconcert the over-rationally minded reader, and has sometimes led commentators to adjust or amend the text. The Psalms were written and recited *coram deo*, before God's presence, and it was easy and natural for the psalmists to move from talking *about* God to talking *to* God, as there was no essential difference between the two. In a sense all the psalms were addressed to God, and it is partly this that gives them their special character within the Hebrew Bible.

What significance should be attached to the fact that the Psalms are addressed to God in this way? On the one hand, it is to be recognised that through their words spoken to God the Psalms give powerful expression to a great variety of human feelings and thoughts, and so have provided a vehicle by which people throughout the ages have presented their own thoughts and needs to him. Whereas scripture as a whole is often thought to be a means by which God speaks to us, in the Psalms it is human beings who speak to God. Thus the Psalms can be said, in the words of Bernhard Anderson,[19] to speak *for* us rather than *to* us. They open up a way for us to speak to God. On the other hand, there have been those who have emphasised that the Psalms, like other parts of scripture, represent God's word to us. In medieval times the Jewish scholar Saadiah Gaon stirred up a lively controversy by arguing that since all the words of scripture are God's words spoken to us, even those words of the Psalms which are apparently addressed to God, are in reality God's words to us, and should be treated as divine rather than human words.[20] But in whatever sense God may be said to speak to us through the words of scripture, it is a mistake to try to make a distinction within the Bible between 'divine' words addressed to us, and 'human' words addressed to God. The whole of the Bible is made up of human words; and if God in some sense 'speaks' to us through the Bible it is through these human words, some of which are prayers addressed to God. In this respect the Psalms are no different from other parts of the Bible: they are human words through which something of God may be encountered.

But there is some special significance in the fact that the Psalms are spoken to God. While it is true that by this direct form of address they do speak for us, and provide a means by which our thoughts and feelings can be opened to God, they do more than that. They give unique expression to some fundamental aspects of the human relationship with God which could not be expressed in any other way. By paying attention to their mode of address to God and to what is said to God in this way, we can learn something about the depths of the human relationship with God. For our purposes, the psalmists' way of addressing God directly offers, as we shall see, a special insight into the question of deliverance from evil, which is a part of our theme.

What follows, then, is a deliberate attempt to interpret the Psalms in a particular way. The central chapters of the book will focus on a variety of poetic images, and the last chapter on the direct address to God, in order to provide an interpretation of the psalmists' understanding of evil and of deliverance from evil. Evil is a mystery, something which cannot be grasped by rational thought, and whose existence and origin no one has been able to explain. But what cannot be comprehended by human reason can in some measure be pictured by the imagination, described in images, understood by the heart and wrestled with in prayer. Poetry and imagery can bring home the reality of evil where rational argument fails. Although we cannot hope to explain evil, we can attempt through images and symbols to understand something about it at a deeper level: to gain some insight into its character, to have a sense of how it affects people, and to discover how we can be delivered from it and protected against it. The prayer-poems of the Psalter give us a unique means of doing this.

Chapter 2

Interpreting the Psalms

To see in the Psalms a way of understanding evil and deliverance is to offer an interpretation. In doing so it is useful to recall that, since the time when they were composed, the Psalms have been understood and interpreted in a great many different ways, and that our interpretation will be only one out of a very large number. There is probably no piece of literature in the world which has been so variously interpreted. New interpretations have arisen not simply because people of different periods and cultures have naturally understood the Psalms differently, but because they have deliberately set out to relate them to the historical and religious situation of their own day. In other words, there has been a constant process, not just of interpretation, but of deliberate re-interpretation of the Psalms. This re-interpretation has had two aspects. It has involved, in the first place, the use of a variety of hermeneutical methods or interpretative techniques: people in different ages have set about the task of interpreting the Psalms in widely differing ways. And this has led, in the second place, to widely differing meanings or religious messages being taken from the Psalms, or, in some cases, being read into them. In this chapter we will look briefly at some of the ways in which the Psalms have been re-interpreted, in order to show that there is no one correct method of interpretation, and no one single strand of meaning to be drawn from the Psalms, and in this way to set the approach adopted here in context.

The Early Period

We can see the beginnings of this process of re-interpretation within the Psalter itself. It is likely that Israelite psalmists took over some pagan or Canaanite poems and re-interpreted and re-applied them to their own culture and religious understandings. Thus Ps. 29 is probably an adaptation of a psalm about the god Baal, and Ps. 19 appears to be an enlargement and re-interpretation of an original poem about the sun.[1] Later, in post-exilic times when there was no longer a king in Israel, a different kind of re-interpretation took place: psalms which spoke of the king were now re-interpreted to refer either to the people as a whole or to a future messiah. It also came to be generally assumed that the Psalms had been written by David, and from their titles it appears many of them were now interpreted in such a way that they referred to events in the life of David.

The New Testament writers were responsible for a further re-interpretation. Since they believed that the Book of Psalms contained prophecies made by David about the future messiah, it was to this book more than to any other in the Old Testament that they turned for evidence that Jesus was the Christ. Certain psalms in particular were applied to events in the life of Jesus, or to the church, or used in support of the Christian message. Christian writers used a variety of interpretative methods. Paul, a Pharisee and a trained scholar, was quite familiar with prevailing rabbinic interpretations and could use standard rabbinic methods for Christian purposes;[2] but he could also offer deliberately new interpretations. For example, the words of Ps. 19:4, 'Their voice has gone out to all the earth', were usually understood to apply to the celestial bodies, but Paul gave them a new meaning by applying them to the work of Christian preachers (Rom. 10:18). The writer to the Hebrews gives an entirely new interpretation of Ps. 110, basing a large part of his teaching about Christ on a detailed analysis of the psalm, and taking the figure of Melchizedek found in it as a type or foreshadowing of Christ. More generally, the Gospels and Acts show that a number of verses from the Psalms were used as proof texts to substantiate Christian belief, and many of them are still read by Christian people as if they apply directly to Christ. The words

You are my son; today I have begotten you. (2:7)

The stone that the builders rejected has become the chief cornerstone. (118:22)

He committed his cause to the LORD; let him deliver him. (22:8, RSV)

For my thirst they gave me vinegar to drink. (69:21)

They divide my clothes among themselves, and for my clothing they cast lots. (22:18)

were all understood by the first Christians to point to the life of Jesus. Insofar as the church of today reads these verses in this way, it is accepting both the method of interpretation adopted by New Testament writers and the meaning which they drew from the Psalms.

Meanwhile Jewish teachers developed their own interpretations. The rabbis of the early centuries of the Common Era believed that every word of scripture had 'seventy aspects', and in their *midrashim* they sought to bring out the hidden or inner meaning of the text. A *midrash*, from the Hebrew verb *d-r-š*, to seek, involves a search into this inner meaning. Traditions of interpretation were developed over a long period, and the words of respected rabbis were preserved and later collected to form the *Midrash on Psalms* or *Midrash Tehillim*.[3] The rabbis' purpose was largely homiletic: the *midrashim* were based on sermons delivered orally to teach or give a moral message. They contain an exposition of the Psalms which 'is always subservient to the thoroughly practical aim of supplying the material for a stirring and edifying discourse'.[4] The principal method used was a distinctive one. It involved linking a text in the Psalter to other verses in the Bible in order to illuminate it or broaden its meaning, using one verse to comment on another. The rabbis juxtaposed verses which were apparently entirely different, 'without regard to context or literal meaning', in the belief that 'the Bible is God's indisputable word and that its every word finds echo and confirmation everywhere else in it.'[5] They were able to do so because of their remarkable familiarity with the text: in Levine's words, 'all of Scripture echoed in their heads'.[6] This method gave scope for a remarkable degree of flexibility and creativity. Since they did not have a concept of one, true, original sense of scripture but believed that scripture was rich in meanings, the rabbis could go in for 'aesthetic creativity', and even for 'embroidery' of the text in order to bring out some aspect of its meaning.[7] So 'by culling out kindred words and expressions from various parts of Scripture and juxtaposing them the Rabbis were often able to achieve a deeper understanding of the particular text with which they dealt.'[8] For example, Ps. 1, which tells of the blessedness of those who walk uprightly, is connected with Ps. 84:11–12, 'No good thing will he withhold from them that walk uprightly. O LORD of hosts, blessed is the man that trusteth in Thee'; which is in turn related first to Abraham, to whom God says 'Walk before Me, and be thou upright' (Gen. 17:1), and then to all who walk before him in uprightness.[9] In this way the psalm is linked both to the Bible story and also to the lives of ordinary people.

Many of these intricate interconnections may not strike home to modern non-Jewish readers, but some of the colourful elaboration of the meaning of words and phrases and the imaginative reference to other parts of scripture can still grip our imagination. As when the *midrash* on Ps. 22:6 ('I am a worm and not human') links the verse with Isa. 41:14 ('Do not fear, you worm Jacob'), and comments:

> Like a worm whose only resource is its mouth, so the children of Israel have no resource other than the prayers of their mouths. Like a worm which roots out a tree with its mouth, so the children of Israel with the prayers of their mouths root out the evil decrees which nations of the earth devise against them.[10]

As time went on Christian writers began to develop a number of other ways in which scripture could be read. This process is associated particularly with the city of Alexandria, and above all with Origen. He believed that scripture had a threefold meaning, corresponding to the human body, soul and spirit, but the principal distinction was between literal and spiritual interpretation. It was possible to understand scripture at the 'bodily' or literal level, but this was the least satisfactory approach. Origen attacked those who understood scripture not 'according to its spiritual meaning', but 'according to the mere letter'. 'To take the language of the Bible "literally" was for him to empty it of all transcendent reference, to confine it to the "corporeal" world.' The hidden meaning of the text was discovered by interpreting the text 'spiritually', that is to say, using allegory and typology. 'Allegory was required to give the biblical text appropriate depth and density of meaning.'[11] There were no criteria for discovering the 'right' meaning of the text: different interpretations were possible, but a 'spiritual' reading gave a richer or deeper meaning than a literal one. This method of interpretation was not universally favoured – scholars at the other great centre of Christian learning at Antioch preferred a more literal approach – but it came to be very widely adopted, and was used as a way of discovering Christ in the Old Testament. So the Psalms were frequently interpreted in what was called the 'spiritual' or 'mystical' sense, that is, allegorically. Regardless of the literal or historical meaning of the text, the words of the Psalms were seen to point to Christ in an allegorical or typological way, and could also be used to provide guidelines for the Christian and spiritual life.

The greatest expositor of the Psalms in the early period was Augustine, whose *Enarrationes* or expository sermons on the Psalms run to six volumes. Augustine accepted that there were two ways of reading the Psalms, the literal and the spiritual, but his emphasis was on the latter. For him the scriptures spoke of Christ, and in the Psalms in particular Christ spoke through the words of David. At the hand of a spiritual giant such as Augustine this method of interpretation could yield expositions of great spiritual depth. The opening words of his discourses on the Psalms show how he relates everything to Christ. The 'man who walks not in the counsel of the wicked' (1:1) 'is to be understood of our Lord Jesus Christ, the Lord Man.' Two verses later, the tree planted by streams of water is also Christ, who will draw people 'into the roots of his discipline' away from the streams of water, that is their sins.[12] Such a method of interpretation may seem strange to many people today, but it yielded results which can enrich our understanding of Christ. And when, for example, he interprets the 'everlasting gates' of Ps. 24:7, 9 as 'entrances of eternal life, of renunciation of the world and conversion to God', or 'doors of everlasting righteousness, of love and chastity',[13] his method of interpreting the Psalms is one which is still used by preachers in our own time.

The Middle Ages and the Reformation

Augustine knew no Hebrew, and his exposition of the Psalms was based on the Latin (Vulgate) translation. This was true also of those who followed in the medieval period. By this time the accepted method of interpretation which began with Origen had been systematised into four levels, sometimes known as the *Quadriga*: the literal, the moral, the allegorical, and the anagogical (or prophetic, that is, what the text is pointing to). Although the principal emphasis remained on the distinction between the allegorical and the literal, this four-fold interpretative scheme was maintained throughout the Middle Ages, and frequently used as a basis for sermons. It also allowed for a great variety of interpretations and for the exercise of human ingenuity. But at the same time there was a strong emphasis on maintaining the orthodoxy of faith, and a sense that there was an 'authoritative interpretation' to which expositors had to conform.[14] So while it was held that 'all the meanings which can be found in scripture by human ingenuity . . . may be taken to have been put there by God', this was true only so long as they were 'consonant with orthodoxy of faith'.[15] Moreover, the continued use of the Vulgate and the lack of access to the Hebrew text limited the ability of medieval expositors to explore the text of the Psalms in detail.

A very different interpretation of the Psalms was developed by a number of distinguished Jewish scholars who flourished between the tenth and thirteenth centuries. The best known among them were Rabbi Saadiah Gaon, Rabbi Solomon Isaac (known as 'Rashi'), Abraham Ibn Ezra, and Rabbi David Kimchi (known as 'Radak'), but there were others as well.

Saadiah, who wrote in Arabic, had learned linguistic, philological and grammatical skills from Muslim scholars which he and those who followed him applied to the study of Hebrew. With the help of this linguistic knowledge they made an accurate study of the Hebrew text of the Psalms, with a view to understanding its original and literal meaning in a way that had not been done before. They retained a respect for the rabbinic tradition, and 'treasured up with pithy brevity the traditions that are interspersed in the Talmud and the Midrash'.[16] But unlike the earlier rabbis with their method of taking single verses or phrases from the text and connecting them with words found elsewhere in scripture, these scholars undertook systematic exposition of the whole text of individual psalms.[17] From our point of view it is interesting to note that although they had much in common, these expositors also held considerably differing, and in some cases new and radical, views about the Psalms and how they should be interpreted.[18]

The greatest of them, Rashi, wrote a popular commentary on the Psalms which is still in use today. In it he not only drew from earlier rabbinic sources, but also used a method known as *peshat* (or 'straightforward'), which was a 'realistic, rationally historical' interpretation,[19] 'drawing on the rational tools of comparative philology and analysis of the historical, literary, and linguistic elements of the text.'[20] As with the earlier rabbis, the purpose of these scholars was partly homiletic: they sought to teach moral lessons which would be relevant to the lives of people of their own day. But they also aimed to encourage and support traditional Jewish beliefs, and to link the Psalms with the later experience of the Jewish people, particularly the experience of exile which they believed to be a continuing feature of the life of Israel, and to their hopes for the future. In doing so they also had a special aim of refuting the claims of Christians that the Psalms pointed to Jesus as the Christ. Thus, in addition to developing a new hermeneutical method, they took from the Psalms a message which was quite different from that taken by Christians of the same period. Alongside homiletic and theological material these commentaries contain spiritual gems, which can speak to people of all periods and traditions. Here, for example, is Rashi offering an expansion of Ps. 5:1 ('Give ear to my words, O LORD; give heed to my sighing'):

> When I have the ability to express my wants before you orally, please hearken to my words. But when fear and worry render me mute and incapable of putting my desires into words, please understand the thoughts sealed up in my heart.[21]

With the theologians of the Reformation we come to yet another approach to the Psalms. As a result of the work of certain humanist scholars who had acquired a knowledge of Hebrew from Jewish sources, the Reformers were now in a position to read the text in the original language, as opposed to the Latin Vulgate, and to attempt to discover its original meaning. They also had access to Jewish interpretations. Since they believed firmly that the Bible was the Word of God and the foundation for all Christian belief and theology, both Luther and Calvin were concerned to base their interpretation on an accurate understanding of what the text meant when it was written. They saw it as their task

> to remove erroneous glosses, such as those supplied by Augustine and other fathers of the Church of Rome, and provide instead interpretations that would be authoritative insofar as they reflected the stated word of God.[22]

This historical approach did not mean that the Reformers were concerned with critical questions as to the authorship and date of the Psalms – they continued to assume that David had composed most of them – but it did involve abandonment of the allegorical method that had been used in the church since New Testament times. This was a new development in the Christian approach to the Psalms. It is true that Luther, like Augustine, recognised a difference between a 'literal' and a 'spiritual' approach, but for him a spiritual approach was a matter not of allegorisation but of seeing pointers to Christ in the Old Testament in general and the prophetic writings in particular.

Like other interpreters before them, the Reformers took their own message from the Psalms. Both Luther and Calvin give profoundly theological interpretations, finding in the Psalms a basis for their own theology, and using them as a means of developing and expounding Reformation teaching. Luther, for example, saw the theology of justification by faith in Ps. 130, which he regarded as 'amongst the most excellent and principal Psalms'. Commenting on the last verse, he says:

> [T]he proud try to find satisfaction and redemption in their own good works, attempt to work their own way out and be their own helper, redeemer and source of mercy. They try to earn themselves truth and righteousness. But what results from these attempts? . . . [G]ood works cannot help. If anyone wants to amount to something before God, he must insist on grace, not on merit.[23]

Thus in spite of their attempt to get back to the original and historical meaning of the Psalms, the Reformers present us with a further re-interpretation which reflects their own theological views and their perception of the spiritual needs of their time.

The Historical-critical Approach

The biggest change in the interpretation of the Psalms came with the emergence of biblical criticism in the nineteenth century. Adopting a rational 'scientific' approach which has come to be called 'historical-critical', Christian, mainly Protestant scholars in the West began to raise new questions about the Psalms, their date and authorship, and the situations out of which they arose. Abandoning the traditional belief that they were mostly written by David, scholars now traced what they believed to be their historical background, frequently attempting to identify particular historical events for which particular psalms were written. They also looked critically at the text of the Psalms, removing what they believed to be glosses or later additions, and dividing up some which seemed originally to have been two discrete poems. One of the questions which was much discussed was that of who the 'I' that we encounter in many of the psalms might be. Many of the scholars of this period believed that a large number of the psalms were in a sense autobiographical: they arose directly out of the experiences of individual people and gave personal accounts of those experiences. But it was not clear who these individuals were, and there was much speculation about the particular circumstances which formed the background of their experiences. Other scholars believed that this 'I' was a representative individual, someone speaking not for himself, but for the community or nation. In keeping with the notion that in ancient society the community was a kind of 'corporate personality', the 'I' of the Psalms could be seen only as 'a figurative description of the nation'.[24]

This 'historical-critical' approach to the Old Testament as a whole, and to the Psalms in particular, has been with us in one way or another ever since, and scholars have tended to assume that earlier, 'pre-critical' interpretations are not worthy of consideration. The questions raised – about the situations out of which the psalms arose, when they were written, and the identity of the individual mentioned in them – have dominated much of the scholarly discussion. But within this general approach new questions were raised during the twentieth century, which have led to a change of emphasis in Psalm studies. Soon after the beginning of the century Herman Gunkel produced his form-critical study of the Psalms. In it he identified a number of types of psalms, mainly on the grounds of their form. The main types were:

- hymns
- communal laments
- royal psalms
- individual laments, and
- individual thanksgivings

but there were also

- psalms of confidence
- communal thanksgivings
- wisdom psalms
- pilgrimage psalms
- liturgies and
- mixed poems

This typology has been broadly accepted by most scholars ever since, and has proved to be very useful. It has formed the basis for further illuminating studies, in particular those of Westermann, who revealed the significant relationship that exists between psalms of lament and psalms of thanksgiving, and showed how a cry for help often moves into an expression of praise.[25]

Following on from this identification of different types of psalms, the Scandinavian scholar Sigmund Mowinckel developed the view that the psalms should be seen as liturgical documents, which were used in the 'cult' – the worship in the temple at Jerusalem.[26] In particular, he argued that the Autumn Festival, the main religious festival of the Israelite calendar, included a celebration of the enthronement of Yhwh as king, and that a considerable number of the psalms were used in connection with this celebration. The human king played an important part in the cult, and the 'I' of the psalms should in many cases be understood to be the king. Some scholars, notably Birkeland, Johnson, Eaton and Croft,[27] went further and came to regard a very large number of the psalms, perhaps almost half the total, as 'royal', including many of the individual and communal laments, as well as thanksgivings and hymns. Some, especially Johnson and Eaton, believed that in the Jerusalem cult a ritual drama took place, as it did in other communities of the ancient Near East, in which the king engaged in a ritual battle with his enemies, and perhaps suffered a ritual humiliation before his victory. These issues have until recently been the main focus of scholarly debate on the Psalms. Most commentaries or other scholarly works written in the twentieth century discuss such questions as the various types of psalms, how they came to be written, and how they were connected with the worship of the temple.

This historical-critical approach has produced a way of looking at and interpreting the Psalms which is very different from the interpretative approaches of earlier centuries. It has many strengths, and has yielded many important insights, not least by providing a clearer understanding of the original meaning of the words of the Psalms, and through relating their theology both to Israelite history and to the thought and ideas of the rest of the Old Testament. It has enabled us to see the Psalms in the context of the life, history and worship of the people of Israel, and so has greatly increased our understanding of them. But this approach is not without its problems and difficulties.[28]

One problem is simply that the historical-critical approach has failed to produce a consensus or agreed conclusion on many points. In spite of the apparent scientific objectivity of this approach, and the assured conviction with which many scholars present the results of their own studies, there is in fact a great diversity in the conclusions reached. There is, of course, general agreement on a number of points. Most scholars would accept the types of psalms, and would agree that many of them were composed for use in the cult. But there is no consensus over some of the large questions which scholars of the historical-critical school set out to answer:

- Who wrote the Psalms?
- When were the various psalms written?[29]
- In what way were individual psalms used in the cult?
- Which psalms are 'royal' and what is the significance of the various references to the king?
- Who are the 'enemies' and why are they referred to so often?
- Who is the 'I' mentioned in a great many psalms?

The fact that there are so many different views on these and other topics makes it difficult to place much confidence in the conclusions of any one scholar, since we know that there are others who see things differently.

This may not seem to matter, were it not for the fact that the historical-critical approach, unlike all earlier approaches, has attempted to provide factual, objective answers to questions of psalm interpretation. The great variety of conclusions reached by scholars merely illustrates the fact that even with a scientific approach the interpretation is very largely dependent on the opinions and assumptions which the interpreter brings to the text. Early biblical critics, for example, can be shown to present a distinctively Protestant, and sometimes anti-Jewish, reading of the Psalms.[30] All of which simply brings us back to the point that there is not, and there cannot be, any one single way of understanding and interpreting the

Psalms, and that the historical-critical approach does not provide all the answers.

Another problem with this approach lies in the assumption that is often made that if we can identify the original setting and reference for a psalm we know what it really *means*. But in fact, what a psalm meant within the religious life of the people at the time when it was written or in later ages, is not defined by or limited to the facts about its original purpose and setting. While a critical historical study of a psalm may illuminate its background and give us a tool to help us understand its religious meaning, it does not of itself tell us what that meaning is. For a true understanding of a psalm it is not sufficient to identify what we believe to be its original setting or what was intended by the original psalmist; we need also to attend to what it has said to generations of other 'psalmists' (in the sense of psalm-users) throughout the centuries. To give an extreme example, it may be true, as some have suggested,[31] that Ps. 23 was written to be spoken by the king during an annual ritual drama, but this gives us no clue to the deep religious meaning of this psalm, which has provided comfort and nourishment to so many people.

One further problem deserves a brief mention, as it is related to the concerns of this book. The attempt to identify the original setting of the various psalms has sometimes led to a very prosaic and pedestrian approach to the Psalms. The rich poetic imagery has been frequently interpreted with unimaginative and sometimes amusing literalness. When they encounter mixed or inconsistent metaphors in a psalm, scholars have concluded that there must be some mistake, forgetting that juxtaposition of perhaps conflicting images is part of the stuff of poetry.[32] The historical-critical approach, for all its usefulness, tends by its very nature towards practical and literal interpretations, and puts less emphasis on the importance of metaphor, symbol and image.

Poetic Truth

Our survey has illustrated the fact that there is no one correct method of interpreting the Psalms, and no one correct strand of meaning to be drawn from them, and that all interpreters have read them in the light of their own assumptions and of the needs of their time. The historical-critical approach represents but one chapter, albeit a unique and important one, in the long and very varied history of the interpretation and re-interpretation of the Psalms. It is important from our point of view to realise that this process of re-interpretation has continued in recent years, and a further chapter is being added to this history. There is now 'a new openness to past interpretations'.[33] In addition, many scholars have begun to concern themselves not so much with the original setting of the Psalms, but simply with the texts as pieces of literature which have come down to us, and which we have before us, regardless of when, why or by whom they were written. To them it is the text itself, and what takes place between the text and the reader which matters. This approach, which can be broadly sub-sumed under the term 'postmodern', has many variations. We need not concern ourselves here with the intricacies of postmodern theory, nor with some of the more radical forms of analysis associated with it such as structuralism or deconstruction.[34] More simply, the focus on the text as a piece of literature enables us to look on the Psalms as poems, or rather as 'prayer-poems', pieces of poetry deliberately and carefully constructed in poetic form.[35] Such an approach need not exclude an appreciation of the historical-critical approach and the insights which have emerged from it. For one of the things we have been learning in recent years is that, as there are many ways of interpreting the Psalms, different approaches can often be held together.[36]

Reading the psalms as poetic texts requires a more explicit ack-nowledgement than is sometimes made that one is offering a subjective interpretation, which brings together the words of the psalms and the viewpoint and life situation of the reader. There is no escape from this, and no apology for it is required. In offering an interpretation of this kind I am following the tradition of re-interpretation of the Psalms which has come down to us through the centuries.

Chapter 3

Poetic Imagery

All language uses images, metaphors and other figures of speech, but poetry makes special use of them, and the Psalms are particularly rich in poetic imagery. Images are expressed in figures of speech. These may be purely decorative, adding interest and colour to what is being said. Similes are often nothing more than this. But a large proportion of the images in the Psalms are in the form of metaphors, and metaphors are often more subtle. Frequently they present us with images which point to something profound which is not immediately obvious. A metaphor has been described as

> an attempt to express in terms of experience thoughts which lie
> beyond experience, to express the abstract in terms of the concrete,
> to picture forth the unfamiliar by means of the familiar, to express
> insensuous thought by sensuous terms.[1]

In other words, images of this kind are a way of seeing things differently. A metaphor can be thought of as a lens[2] which is offered to us to give us a changed perspective on an aspect of reality. Poetic images, not least the images found in the Psalms, can enable us to see something beyond, some truth which lies below the surface of everyday reality. A poetic image

> . . . convey[s] to our imagination something more than the accurate
> reflection of an external reality . . . It looks out from a mirror in
> which life perceives not so much its face as some truth about its
> face.[3]

Poetic images are not a kind of code. An image does not stand for one thing only, the same thing all the time. Images 'are affected by the emotional vibrations of their context, so that each reader's response to them is apt to be modified by his personal experience'.[4] This happens because metaphors are not always transparent. They not only clarify but also obscure. Their function is to darken as well as to shed light. If they are to be a lens through which we see things differently, they require an exercise of imagination on the part of the reader. They challenge the reader to discern things which are not readily apparent, and become aware of dimensions of things which cannot be given expression in rational prose. When the psalmist calls God a rock we cannot say simply and unequivocally what the image indicates. When he prays, 'Guard me as the apple of the eye' we can attempt to give the meaning of the metaphor by explaining what the phrase 'apple of the eye' refers to; but by doing so we do not penetrate the truth which the image is conveying. If we say that the 'pit' was for the psalmist an image of death we do not communicate the power of the image or the depth of feeling which is at its heart. The metaphors deliberately convey something which is obscure, a meaning which we do not easily see. To grasp the meaning we need to match the image with our own imagination, and to allow our feelings to enter the feeling hidden within it.

It is, of course, possible to interpret a metaphor literally, and this happens more readily in circumstances where it is not absolutely certain whether or not the poet is speaking metaphorically, as is not infrequently the case in the Psalms. As we shall see, the 'enemies', the 'pit', and the 'many waters' can be, and have been, interpreted literally. When the psalmist refers to his eye wasting away, or to being in prison, or even to eating ashes for bread, we can if we wish assume that he is speaking of physical reality. But it may well be that if we take these and many other phrases as metaphors conveying poetic images we will discover depths of meaning which are not present on the surface. We also find that we need not concern ourselves about many of the apparent inconsistencies and contradictions in the Psalms. In a poem which is not a literal and sequential account of a person's experience it is possible to find conflicting images juxtaposed. It is part of the nature of poetry that contradictory thoughts and images can be held together within a larger truth. 'We are in a world', says Cecil Day Lewis, 'where contradictions vanish, fused into one by the passion with which they have been felt'.[5] So when Ps. 13 says 'How long, O LORD? Will you forget me forever?', and a few lines later, 'I will sing to the LORD because he has dealt bountifully with me,' we need not try to explain away the contradiction but look for the larger truth of which both statements are a part.

The possibility of deeper meanings exists particularly with those

metaphors which convey archetypal images. According to Jung, an archetype is a kind of 'primordial image', part of a pattern which exists deep
within the human unconscious. He describes archetypes as 'psychic
residua of numberless experiences of the same type'.[6] They are 'the
imprints preserved in the great memory of innumerable repetitions of
certain modes of experience'.[7] Archetypes can be said to 'express themselves' in the form of images or symbols.[8] Or, to say the same thing the
other way round, images which are felt to be powerful and which move us
at a deep level do so because they represent archetypes. By putting us in
touch with aspects of the archetypal structure of the human psyche they
can stir our feelings, and give rise to thoughts whose origins remain
unknown to us. In a sense 'all psychic imagery partakes of the archetypal
to some extent'[9] but there are certain images which seem to be archetypal
in a special way, which can stir us more powerfully than their surface
meaning might suggest. Many of these tend to appear frequently in poetry.
Images of the night, the sea or forests, snakes or dragons, caves or pits,
mountains or roses can all touch our feelings in inexplicable ways. Such
images, if used by a poet in expressive language, can touch 'depths not
measurable by the gauges of normal experience, glimpses of "caverns
measureless to man"'.[10] That is to say, they have the potential to convey to
us something that is transcendental, beyond us and of another world, and
which cannot be reached by the processes of logical reasoning. Many of
the images found in the Psalms are of this kind, as we shall see.

The Psalm images have another characteristic: many of them are
'conventional' rather that original. That is to say, they are found repeated
in several psalms, and may well have been standard or stock images
within the religious language of the time. Images of God as a rock, of the
shadow of God's wings, of the pit, or of snares and traps are used
frequently and may be described as conventional. This may suggest that
they have lost their original freshness and expressive power. It is, of
course, true that in the normal course of linguistic development original
and living metaphors can be repeated and reiterated to the extent that they
become stock and eventually dead metaphors.[11] But not all conventional
and reiterated metaphors lose their living quality. Poetry in the ancient
world frequently involved the imaginative re-use of conventional images.
Far from restricting or inhibiting poets, convention of this kind can
provide them with 'a solid framework in which to construct their own
discourse'.[12] The power of this poetry lies in the way the poet uses conventional images, and relocates them in the context of a new poem, which
can then become 'a fine recasting of the conventional'.[13] This is especially

true if the images have powerful archetypal associations in the way described above. They can then have what Cecil Day Lewis calls 'a permanent right-of-way through our hearts':[14] if used imaginatively they can stir our feelings no matter how often they are used. Poetry in which such recurring metaphors are found can be some of the best poetry, and this is especially true of the Psalms. Of course not all the metaphors found there are conventional or repeated. Some of the best known images in the Psalter occur only once: 'Guard me as the apple of the eye' (17:8); 'Cast your burden on the LORD' (55:22). But in a special way 'the Book of Psalms is the showcase for the artful use of . . . stock images.'[15]

This use of conventional imagery suggests that in the main the Psalms were not composed in connection with specific events in history or in the personal experience of the psalmist, which we can then hope to discover by careful study and research. In spite of the references to events in the life of David in the superscription of a number of psalms, and the attempts by some scholars to identify particular historical events lying behind them, it is now widely believed that most of the psalms do not refer to particular identifiable situations, but rather to typical situations which can occur and recur in the lives of individuals or of the people. They were written in such a way that they could be read with reference to a variety of events or circumstances. For this purpose conventional and familiar phrases and images were particularly suitable, because they allowed users of the psalms to identify with the thoughts and feelings expressed in them, and to understand them in relation to their own circumstances. In addition, the archetypal character of much of the imagery, by the very fact that it is grounded in feelings which lie underneath the surface of all human life, gives the Psalms a universal application. So for example sickness or disease can be used as a universal image of distress. A psalm like Ps. 22, which describes a situation of extreme discomfort, can be taken to refer not to the troubles of one particular person, but to any distress. The 'I' of the individual psalms can be seen not as an identifiable individual, but, in Mowinckel's phrase, as 'Everyman'.

That is not to say that the feelings expressed by means of these images were unreal, and the imagery was artificial and contrived. The way in which the images are woven into the texture of the psalms makes it clear that the emotions were real and truly felt. Behind the conventional language there lies genuine feeling. The stock images are used to express actual experience. It is in this way that people of different kinds and in a variety of situations can make this imagery their own, and feel it to be an expression of their own feelings and needs.

That such a general application of the Psalms was intended from the start becomes more apparent when we remember that they were written for liturgical use. Just how and by what kind of people they were written we do not know. Some may have been composed by 'cultic prophets' connected with the temple from an early period.[16] Or it may be that many were produced by guilds of Levites who were responsible for the temple.[17] But however they were produced, most of them were probably composed as liturgical poems for use in the temple cult. Now one of the characteristics of liturgy is that it uses general language in such a way that worshippers can individually and collectively identify with the thoughts and feelings expressed, and apply them to their own situations. Through the deliberately non-specific phraseology of the liturgy people can bring their own situations before God, and express their own feelings. This seems to have been the way in which people used the Psalms. National psalms, composed perhaps for some special occasion, could be used as corporate liturgies at other times. The individual laments and thanksgivings were a means by which individual worshippers presented their personal needs and responses to God, the conventional imagery providing a vehicle for individual petitions, desires and thanksgivings of various kinds. And even those psalms which may have been originally connected with royal ceremonies or occasions of one kind or another were probably later 'democratised' and used by ordinary individuals or by the community. So as Kraus has said, the worshippers

> learned to give voice to their troubles and thanksgivings in
> language that was able to express their situation fully because it
> transcended each person's own destiny, but which yet, with the use
> of archetypal expressions of suffering and deliverance, could
> portray concrete events vividly, reflect their reality, and give a full
> summation.[18]

The implication of this for later interpreters and users of the Psalms is clear. The images can be regarded as 'open metaphors' which are 'capable of coming to actualisation in many contexts'.[19] Because of the nature of the imagery the Psalms are open to a variety of applications within the life of people today. There is no single fixed meaning. The task of the interpreter is not to establish and lay down the meaning of the psalm, but to illuminate the imagery, perhaps by referring among other things to its probable original setting, in such a way that people are encouraged to discover its relevance to their lives in a variety of ways. As with all poetry, it is for the imagination to discover contexts and situations to which the images can apply. It is because the Psalms can be approached in this way that they have continued to nourish people of faith throughout the centuries.

Nevertheless, beyond this there lies a further possibility. It may be that the imagery of the Psalms does not only allow a variety of applications, but also points to something more inexpressible, more mysterious, which lies behind the world of everyday experience. It is part of the function of poetic images to convey, or at least to hint at, realities which cannot be described in rational prose. A metaphor brings two things together. It illuminates one thing by linking it with another. There is the superficial reference and the hidden reference – in the jargon of linguistics, the 'vehicle' and the 'tenor'. But in linking these two it may also point to a third reality, and hint at a realm beyond the things being referred to. There can be a 'third thing which in logic does not exist'.[20] Images, especially if they are primordial or archetypal, can have what Jung called a 'transcendent function',[21] speaking to us of a mystery. Could it be that the images we find in the Psalms reveal something about the mystery of evil and of deliverance from evil? This is the question we will be pursuing in the following chapters.

The Language of Myth

As a preliminary to this, two further questions should be raised about the images in the Psalms: Do they have their origin in myth? And if so, do we need to explore the myths from which they arise in order to understand the images? The meaning of the word 'myth' is a complicated and controversial question, and there are many different views and definitions.[22] But it is generally recognised that for the people of the ancient civilisations myths were 'an attempt to explain things',[23] a means of interpreting the world and reality. Myths provided an explanation of how the world came to be. In Babylon the creation myth told how the god Marduk overcame the sea monster Tiamat who represented original chaos, and created the world by dividing her corpse in two and spreading it out to form the sky and the earth. Similarly in Canaan, the stories of the defeat of the sea monster Yamm, representing primeval chaos, and of the earth monster Mot, or Death, by the god Baal and his consort Anat are cosmogonic myths telling of the creation of the universe. Myths also explained other aspects of the world and life, such as the rhythm of the seasons, as in the Greek myth of Demeter and Persephone, or the Canaanite myth of the death of Tammuz or Adonis. Some of these myths were enacted in elaborate annual rituals which were believed to ensure the stability of the world, the overcoming of the forces of chaos, and the fertility of the earth and of living creatures. Thus at the New Year festival at Babylon the king took part in the enacting of the myth in a ritual drama which included the overcoming of the forces of evil in a ritual battle, the ritual humiliation of the king representing the dying and rebirth of nature, and a 'sacred marriage' to ensure fertility in the year to come.

In the light of this, one way of understanding myth is to regard it as closely linked with ritual, a view held at one time especially by the so-called 'Myth and Ritual' school of scholars. Myth can be seen as 'the story which the ritual enacts'.[24] The ritual re-enacting of the myths secured the continuity and safety of the world and life, and the well-being of the people. 'Myth is a form by which the existing structure of reality is understood and maintained . . . Existing world order is maintained through the actualisation of the myth in the cult.'[25] In this view,

> Myth is more than merely early man's way of expressing his
> comprehension of the world; it is also what brings the world into
> being – the myth has to be recited, because this is the only means
> of countering the perils which everywhere beset the fixed orders of
> creation, and of guaranteeing their continued existence.[26]

If myth is defined in this way it is understandable that many biblical scholars have been keen to argue that there is no myth in the Old Testament. The people of Israel had their own stories of creation but these were not myths which were ritually enacted. They felt no need to explain and sustain the world through myth and ritual. They explained it with reference to the free actions of a personal God who brought the world into being and directed the course of history. Their stories were part of the *heilsgeschichte*, the history of salvation. If this is so, then it can justifiably be argued that one of the distinctive features of the life of Israelite people was that they rejected myth. Israel was, according to von Rad, 'absolutely unique in taking man out of the sphere of myth'.[27] 'Mythical notions,' says Birkeland, 'did not as a rule survive.'[28]

More recently, however, and partly as a result of archaeological discoveries in ancient Canaan, scholars have tended to take a different view. While it is no doubt true that Israel did not explain the world and seek to sustain its life through the ritual enactment of myths, recent studies have shown that the religion of Israel grew in part out of the myth-based religion of Canaan.[29] 'Israel's religion in its beginning stood in a clear line of continuity with the mythopoeic patterns of West Semitic, especially Canaanite myth.'[30] So it may be appropriate to look for mythical elements in some of the narrative and poetic material of the Old Testament, or to say that some of the Bible stories are in some sense myths. This is a controversial issue which need not concern us here. What is of interest to us is that there are many echoes of ancient, extra-biblical, near eastern myths in the imagery of the Old Testament.[31] We do not know just how familiar these myths may have been to the Israelites of biblical times, and what significance was attached to them. But some of the images in the Psalms in particular clearly refer to, or at least reflect, the language of some of these old myths, particularly Canaanite ones. There are, for example, references to mythical dragons or monsters of the deep – Rahab (89:10) and Leviathan (74:14; 104:26). The images of the sea, waters and floods, of death and Sheol, and possibly the images of wild beasts also seem to have a background in myth. The significance of particular myth-based images will be discussed in detail later. But three brief, general points can be made here about the way in which ancient mythical language is used in the Psalms and some other parts of the Old Testament, which may help our understanding of the particular images when we come to them.

First, the language of myth was frequently used simply as a source of image and metaphor. Even after the myths had ceased to be current within the religious and cultural life of the people, images and metaphors arising from them continued to be used within religious poetry. It may be that, as Mowinckel maintained,[32] this was simply a 'style of writing'. Or it may be that, just because the myths had been current for so long in the near eastern cultures, mythical images continued to have emotive power, and that in this way myth provided 'a fund of powerful emotive language on which creative thinkers could draw'.[33] It would appear, from the way that myth-based images are used in the Psalms and by the authors of Job and Deutero-Isaiah, that for biblical writers the language of myth had been 'liberated'. The biblical poets could 'make free use of the ancient images without being bound by the structure of the myth'.[34] They could draw on the emotive power of mythical language even after the myths as a whole had ceased to retain their explanatory or life-sustaining power.

Secondly, myth-based images were used to symbolise something transcendent. The ancient myths were not just stories, but a way of expressing the meaning of life. They pointed beyond themselves to realities which were felt to be mysterious and otherworldly. They spoke of gods, of super-human agencies, of dark and dreadful forces and of mysterious events which gave birth to the cosmos and controlled its life. So when, as in Israel, the myths no longer provided the explanation of the origin of the cosmos, and were not used in ritual ceremonies to ensure the fertility of life, and when people no longer believed in the gods of the myths, the language of myth still retained powerful connotations of the transcendent. It still spoke to the people of a dimension of life beyond their own every-day existence. Myth-based images still retained what Kraus has called 'traits of transcendence'.[35] Their emotive power lay not only in their deep cultural roots, but, more importantly from our point of view, in their original transcendent reference and meaning.

Thirdly, Israelites began to use the language of myth in a special way, by connecting it with events which they believed to have taken place in their own history. Stories of the overcoming of the primeval waters of chaos and the dragon of the sea, which in the original myths referred to the creation of the world, were applied to the splitting of the Red Sea and the holding back of the waters at the Exodus from Egypt (Ps. 74:12–14; 77:16–20). When Deutero-Isaiah wanted to describe the supreme power of God to control the nations and bring back his people from exile, he drew on the myth of God's victory over the dragon of the deep (Isa. 51:9–11). That is to say, the myths were historicised. They were used not to explain how the world began, but to give an interpretation of the Israelites' own history. The language of myth provided a means of expressing the belief that God acted through historical events. It was a language which creative writers could use 'to lead their people into ever deepening appreciation of the significance of the national history'.[36]

So the language of myth, by its cultural depth and its transcendent reference, carried with it certain depths of meaning. Images which recalled the ancient myths resonated with things deeply embedded below the surface of people's minds, and could thus be particularly powerful. Moreover they could be reinterpreted, and applied to other things, such as events in Israel's history, to add a dimension of transcendence or of depth to them. As we turn to a more detailed look at the poetic images of the Psalms, we should pay particular attention to those images which have their source in myth, and look for layers of meaning in them which are not apparent if they are looked at superficially.

Chapter 4

Evil and Distress

The psalmists did not, of course, speak only in images: they used non-figurative language as well. As we turn now to the theme of evil and distress, it will be useful first to look at some of the ordinary, non-figurative words they used, to see what they tell us about the psalmists' understanding of evil. There are two principal Hebrew words which convey the idea of evil, *ra'* (or the feminine form *rā'āh*) and *'āwen*. The first of these is much more common, being found in one or other of its forms (masculine and feminine) over 600 times in the Old Testament. It is used with various shades of meaning, and so is rendered by a number of English words. In the New Revised Standard Version of the Psalms it usually appears as 'evil', but is sometimes translated as 'mischief', 'wickedness', 'trouble', 'adversity', 'affliction' or 'hurt'. It is a theologically important word, but it has received surprisingly little attention from leading theologians of the Old Testament.[1]

In the Psalms, where the word *ra'* (or *rā'āh*) is used some 60 times, it does not usually refer directly to evil as a superhuman power, but to the outworkings of that power in human life. It has two principal meanings, which to our modern minds seem to be distinct and separate, but which in the context of the Old Testament appear to overlap and to be sometimes indistinguishable.[2] To focus initially on the first of these meanings, *ra'* refers to evil in the sense of moral evil or wickedness. It is the opposite of good: 'Depart from evil and do good' (37:27); 'You love evil more than good' (52:3). It is something which can characterise human behaviour, but at the same time it appears to be something which exists independently of human beings. It cannot, however, exist in the presence of God: 'Evil will not sojourn with you' (5:4). The righteous will therefore hate evil (97:10), reject it (36:4), keep their tongue from it (34:13), and hold back their feet from every evil way (119:101). By contrast, the wicked have an evil purpose (64:5), have evil thoughts and intentions (56:5), repay evil for good (35:12; 38:20; 109:5), and give their mouths free reign for evil (50:19). Although it is a power external to humans, it is also something that people *do*. The psalmist confesses that he has 'done what is evil in your sight' (51:4). The blameless are those who 'do no evil to their friends' (15:3). *Ra'* is used with reference to 'wicked deeds' (141:5), or simply 'wickedness' (94:23; 107:34). More specifically, it causes people to devise evil against other people, or inflict evil on them (21:11; 41:7; 56:5; 64:5). The wicked are those who are enticed into behaviour of this kind, whereas the righteous will spurn evil and depart from it.

This sense that evil is moral wickedness in which humans can become involved is deepened by the other Hebrew word used, *'āwen*. This is a fairly uncommon word, frequently translated 'iniquity', but it could also be rendered as 'viciousness'. It is often found in parallel or in association with other words, usually 'the wicked' (*rešā'îm*), 'mischief' (*'āmāl*), or 'evil' (*ra'*). It is a mysterious word, having overtones of something sinister and perhaps demonic. It is 'the abyss of viciousness'.[3] It conveys the sense that there is something evil outside human beings which can take them over. It can play havoc with the life of a community, as when one psalmist observes:

> Iniquity [*'āwen*] and trouble are within it,
> ruin is in its midst. (55:10f).

Or it can threaten to dominate the life of the individual person, causing another psalmist to pray: 'Never let iniquity have dominion over me' (119:133). Those who are taken over by evil and become enmeshed in it are 'workers of iniquity' or 'evildoers' (*pō'alê 'āwen*), a phrase which refers possibly to sorcerers, but certainly to vicious, deceitful and potentially dangerous characters. They are 'bloodthirsty' (59:2) and 'scheming' (64:2) people, who 'speak peace with their neighbours, while mischief is in their hearts' (28:3), who lay snares (141:9) and 'eat up' God's people 'as they eat bread' (14:4). The word (*'āwen*), therefore, refers to the moral evil to which the word *ra'* alludes, but suggests that it is something deep, mysterious, vicious and dangerous, in which humans can get caught up. Both words imply that evil is a power external to humans which leads people into wicked deeds and vicious, deceitful behaviour.

But there is a second strand of meaning in the word *ra'*. As well as referring to wicked deeds and thoughts, it can refer to calamity, disaster, trouble or affliction, and can be translated in a variety of ways:

Throughout all generations we shall not meet *adversity*. (10:6)

Many are the *afflictions* of the righteous. (34:19)

Let all those who rejoice at my *calamity*
   be put to shame and confusion. (35:26)

Not infrequently it is used of times of suffering, famine or disaster. The righteous

. . . are not put to shame in evil times,
in the days of famine they have abundance. (37:19)

The LORD will give them 'respite from days of trouble' (94:13), so that they have no need to be afraid of 'times of trouble' (49:5), or of 'evil tidings' (112:7). They can 'fear no evil' (23:4), and be confident that 'no evil shall befall' them (91:10).

Sometimes it is not clear which of the two meanings is intended, moral evil or affliction. When Ps. 40 laments that

evils have encompassed me
   without number; . . .
my iniquities have overtaken me,
   until I cannot see. (v. 12)

the 'evils' may be seen as either iniquities or misfortunes. When enemies are said to 'plan evil' (21:11) or 'devise evil' (35:4) against the psalmist, does this refer to the wickedness of their plans, or to the harm they intend to bring upon their victim? When the assurance is given that 'The LORD will keep you from all evil' (121:7), and that 'no evil shall befall you' (91:10), is the psalmist promising freedom from moral evil or from disaster and affliction? From these examples it is apparent that the two meanings overlap, and that the psalmists do not make a clear distinction between moral evil and disaster or calamity. Wickedness and affliction seem to be combined within one concept, without it being clear how these two are related to one another. Evil, as represented by the word *ra'* is, therefore, a broad concept, referring to a range of human suffering and wrong.

The key to understanding this is that the calamities or disasters re-presented by the word *ra'* were seen as products of the power of evil. They were no ordinary or trivial misfortunes or difficulties. Like wicked deeds and thoughts, these forms of suffering were felt to be brought about by a mysterious, superhuman power. The very inexplicable nature of human suffering, the lack of any answer to the question 'Why?', can lead people to attribute it to something uncontrollable beyond themselves. It was no doubt for this reason that sickness of all kinds came to be attributed to superhuman powers, as when Ps. 91:6 talks of 'the pestilence that stalks in darkness', or Ps. 78:49 of the 'company of destroying angels' bringing plague; or when Ps. 22:12–17 speaks in the same context of symptoms of illness and of demonic wild beasts.[4] Sickness was seen as a 'total threat' to a person's existence,[5] an encroachment of Sheol, the place of separation from God. All such affliction – sickness, tragedy, pestilence and the afflictions of war – was a form of *ra'*, leading to death. *Ra'* in the form either of affliction or of slavery to wicked ways could drag people down to Sheol. It is not surprising, therefore, that the psalmists did not always distinguish between the two forms of evil.

Distress

What the psalmists say about distress, therefore, can tell us something about their understanding of evil. The Psalms are full of references to troubles, difficulties and distress. These are found throughout the Psalter, but especially in what we may call the 'prayer psalms', that is to say, those in which God is addressed in the second person, as 'Thou' or 'You', either throughout the psalm or in a large part of it. These include a few 'hymns' and some 'psalms of thanksgiving'; but the larger number are psalms of complaint or lament, either 'laments of the individual' or 'laments of the community'. In them the psalmist calls out to God from the midst of trouble, and in many cases then moves on to thank God for his deliverance.

These psalms refer to distress in a variety of ways. We find a large number of ordinary words which refer to the subjective experience of suffering or distress in a general and largely non-metaphorical way. In the personal prayer psalms there are more than 20 nouns referring to trouble of one kind or another. The most common of these are the twin words *ṣar* and *ṣārāh*, meaning trouble or distress in a very general way. A stronger word, usually translated 'affliction' (*'oni*), is also fairly common. In addition there are words which refer to grief, sorrow, weeping or tears, to different degrees of fear, trembling or dread, to groaning or sighing, and to pain, distress, anguish or sorrow of various kinds. There are significant verbs too, frequently used in the niphal, the passive or reflexive form of the Hebrew verb. The psalmists speak of being dismayed, disturbed, finished, disquieted, forlorn, broken or crushed. Altogether these words make up a rich and varied vocabulary which was used to express feelings of distress of all kinds.

The frequency and variety of these words, and the fact that some of them are very strong, make it clear that in general the psalmists are not referring to slight or trivial difficulties, but to extreme situations of distress, or to strong feelings of pain or fear. Even the common word *ṣar* carries the sense of being restricted or cramped, and can speak of something powerful – what Kraus calls 'the oppression which chokes off life'.[6] Other words also refer to sufferings of a terrible kind. A number of words connected with the verb *d-k-'* or *d-k-h* 'to crush' express a particularly strong feeling of distress. Some psalms in particular, such as 6, 22, 38, 69, 88, and 102, give us the feeling that the poet concerned is struggling to find words to express an anguish of an indescribable kind. Behind the words of the psalm there is what Luther called a 'great affliction' which the psalmist 'cannot adequately describe'.[7] As Broyles says, 'Everything happens in the most extreme form imaginable.'[8]

Because the distress was so acute and so inexpressible, the psalmists naturally turned to poetic images in an attempt to describe their condition. Nowhere do the psalmists tell us exactly what the trouble is or what has caused it. They prefer to speak in metaphor and image. As we have seen, it is a mistake to look on the psalms as autobiography, and to read their metaphors as if they give a literal description of the situation the particular poet was in. To do so is to lose much of their depth and meaning. The use of poetic image not only allows users of the psalm to apply it to their own situation of distress, but also opens windows through which deeper meanings can be seen. The images they use are of different kinds. There are some which describe subjective feelings of suffering by referring to parts of the physical body, and it is worth pausing to look at some of these because they give particularly vivid and powerful expression to the psalmists' acute sense of distress.

Bodily Images

It is well known that, for the Hebrews, mind and body were closely interrelated, and that emotions of various kinds were associated with particular parts of the body. It is impossible to tell whether the composer of a psalm was experiencing actual physical pain at the time of writing. It is more meaningful to take these references metaphorically than to attempt to work out what the psalmist's physical ailment may have been.

One common image is that of a person's *bones*. They are the frame that holds the body together. As the medieval Jewish scholars recognised, the bones 'symbolise the entire body because they are its mainstay'[9] 'Bones' can therefore be used as a synonym for 'body', or for a person's whole being. When the psalm says 'All my bones shall say, "O LORD, who is like you?"'(35:10), it refers to the psalmist's whole person. But the bones are also 'a man's most durable part – his core, so to speak. So long as bones are intact, even a dead man retains a minimal existence.'[10] So they stand for a person's strength or vitality. When the poet of Ps. 32 says,

> While I kept silence, my body [literally, 'bones'] wasted away
>   through my groaning all the day long. (v. 3)

he is expressing a feeling that all of his strength was being sapped, and the last vestiges of life were ebbing away. In addition the bones were understood to be the seat of pain. In Ps. 42:11 the taunts of the enemy were experienced as a 'shattering' or a 'breaking up' of his bones; they felt like a 'deadly wound' threatening his very existence.

Another potent image is that of the *eye*, which could be used with reference to distress both of body and mind. The eye was regarded both as a 'barometer of vitality', and as a 'mirror of both one's misery and happiness'.[11] Strength and vitality of body and mind made the eye bright; weakness made it dim. When the psalmist says, 'My strength fails me; as for the light of my eyes – it has gone from me' (38:10), he is referring to a loss of vitality and strength which have deprived his eyes of their sparkle. The words 'My eyes waste away because of grief', found in Ps. 6:7 and again in Ps. 31:9, are a way both of describing the acuteness of a person's sorrow, and also of saying that strength and vitality were draining away. 'My eyes grow dim with waiting for my God' (69:3) is 'a picturesque way of describing one's exhaustion, both mental and physical'.[12] Used in this way, the eye could be a powerful metaphor for distress.

Then we have the frequent reference to *tears* or weeping. Here especially it is impossible to say whether the psalmists are speaking literally or metaphorically. Sometimes these words are simply a powerful and fairly literal way of referring to distress and grief:

> Do not hold your peace at my tears. (39:12)

> The LORD has heard the sound of my weeping. (6:8)

> You have delivered . . . my eyes from tears. (116:8)

But at other times they are used more metaphorically, to form part of an imaginative picture:

My tears have been my food day and night. (42:3)

You have fed them with the bread of tears,
  and given them tears to drink in full measure. (80:5)

You have . . . put my tears in your bottle. (56:8)

Finally, we should notice the images of being *parched* or *withered*, and of *thirst*. This language too can be used in different ways. It can describe the feeling of continuing and unremitting distress:

I am weary with my crying:
  my throat is parched. (69:3)

It can also express a sense of wasting away, of life coming to an end. 'As grass withers in the heat, so the innermost being of the sufferer dries up.'[13]

My heart is stricken and withered like grass;
  I am too wasted to eat my bread.

My days are like an evening shadow;
  I wither away like grass. (102:4, 11)

And because dryness brings a thirst or longing for water, the image is used to express not only distress but also the longing for God:

O God, you are my God, I seek you,
  my soul thirsts for you;
my flesh faints for you,
  as in a dry and weary land where there is no water. (63:1)

I stretch out my hands to you;
  my soul thirsts for you like a parched land. (143:6)

The longing for God is experienced as a kind of distress. 'The soul's thirst for God', says the medieval Jewish commentator Radak, 'is even more intense than the body's craving for water.'[14] This image links the experience of distress with a sense of the absence of God, giving us the hint of a point we shall return to later.

These and other references to parts of the body (loins, 38:7; tongue, 22:15), are a way of painting a picture of extreme pain and distress. Taken together with the variety of general words for trouble, they serve to emphasise the acuteness of the affliction to which the psalmists were referring. These images give very vivid expression to what people were feeling. But in addition to the bodily images, there are others which are of a different character: images which say something not simply about the experience of suffering but about the nature of the trouble or distress and how it came about. It is these images which may tell us more about the psalmists' understanding of evil. As we have seen, distress and suffering was a form of *ra'*; it was produced by a power which caused both human suffering and human wickedness. We may assume, therefore, that in presenting images which point to the character and origin of their distress they are saying something also about the power of evil which brought about both human affliction and human wickedness. So for a fuller understanding of the psalmists' view of evil we need to look more closely at these images.

Evil Caused by God?

But before we do so there is one further point about *ra'* which deserves attention: namely, that it was sometimes apparently brought about by God himself. This is seldom stated directly in the Psalms, although the poets of Pss 42 and 88 attribute their waves or floods of affliction to God (42:7 and 88:15f),[15] and a similar thought may be implied in 55:5, 78:49 and 90:15. The idea is found more frequently elsewhere in the Old Testament, especially in the Deuteronomistic writings, where God himself is said to bring *ra'* upon his people:

> Therefore I will bring evil [*ra'*] upon the house of Jeroboam.
> (1 Kings 14:10)

> I will bring disaster [*ra'*] on you. (1 Kings 21:21)

> I am bringing upon Jerusalem and Judah such evil [*ra'*] that the ears of everyone who hears of it will tingle. (2 Kings 21:12)

More remarkable still are some words in the prophets:

> Does disaster [*rā'āh*] befall a city,
>   unless the LORD has done it? (Amos 3:6)

> I am the LORD . . .
> I form light and create darkness,
>   I make weal and create woe [*ra'*]. (Isa. 45:5, 7)

It should be clear that nowhere is God being accused of being responsible for *ra'* in the sense of moral evil;[16] but apparently God could cause *ra'* in the sense of affliction or disaster.

Sometimes this could be explained in terms of God's punishment. When God said to David after his sin against Uriah, 'I will raise up trouble (*rā'āh*) against you from within your own house' (2 Sam. 12:11), this was clearly intended as a punishment; and the same is true of the verses from 1 and 2 Kings quoted above. The Deuteronomists in particular believed that God punished his people for their rebellion, and they interpreted personal and national disasters in this way. But there were other times when affliction seemed to have been caused by God for no apparent reason. Trouble (*rā'āh*) could be said simply to come 'from the LORD' (2 Kings 6:33). The people could feel themselves to be defeated, rejected and abased by God even when they had committed no fault (44:9–17). God seemed sometimes to inflict *ra'* upon people in an unaccountable and inexplicable way.

This strange activity of God found a special expression in one of the images we will discuss, that of God hiding his face. When he did so he withdrew his presence and separated himself from people, so that they were cut off and forsaken. In these circumstances it seemed that God himself was bringing about the condition of God-forsakenness which was the goal and object of the forces of evil. God seemed to be implicated in and responsible for the very evil from which they sought his deliverance. At the every least he appeared by his absence to consent to this evil and let his people be exposed to it;[17] and at times by his withdrawal he seemed directly to cause it (30:7; 104:29). How this could be remained an unsearchable mystery for the psalmists. Nevertheless, one powerful and important point stands out about the attitude of the psalmists to this. If they sometimes felt that evil, at least in the form of human suffering, was being caused by God, they also felt that there was here a gross and insurmountable contradiction. For God to be implicated in evil was impossible; it was against his very nature. In these circumstances all they could do was to cry out to God in protest – to cry to God against God, to complain and appeal to him against what appeared to be happening in his name.[18] The cries, 'Why do you hide your face?' (44:24; 88:14), 'Do not hide your face' (27:9; 69:17; 102:2; 143:7), and 'How long will you hide your face?' (13:1) are not uttered only as calls for help, but as cries of puzzled protest against the utterly incomprehensible situation in which the ultimate evil of separation from God seems to be caused by God himself. For the psalmists evil remained a mystery, which they could neither understand nor confront directly, but whose effects they encountered in the form of suffering. All they could do was to refer to it obliquely or figuratively, using metaphors and images based largely on their experience of distress.

Chapter 5

Images of Distress: (1) Hostility

We turn now to the main body of images we are concerned with, those that say something about the nature of the trouble or distress and how it has come about. Here we are faced with a wide variety of metaphors and images, which can be grouped into three clusters; the first, which we discuss in this chapter, has to do with enmity or hostility; the second and third, which we deal with in the following two chapters, have to do with sinking or being overwhelmed, and with separation or being abandoned.

Enemies

There are three images within this first cluster. The first is that of *enemies*. No one reading the Psalms can fail to be struck by how often they speak of enemies or foes. If we simply thumb through the first few pages of the Psalter we immediately find examples:

> O LORD, how many are my foes!
>   Many are rising against me. (3:1)

> Lead me, O LORD, in your righteousness
>   because of my enemies. (5:8)

> All my enemies shall be ashamed and struck with terror;
>   they shall turn back, and in a moment be put to shame. (6:10)

> Rise up, O LORD, in your anger;
>   lift yourself up against the fury of my enemies. (7:6)

The most common and ordinary Hebrew word for an enemy, *'ōyēb*, occurs no fewer than 72 times in the Psalter, including 26 times in individual laments. A pair of related words, often translated 'adversary', is also fairly common; and there are others which mean literally 'those who persecute me', 'those who watch for me', 'those who hate me' and 'those who rise up against me' – all verbal participles in Hebrew, which are sometimes used in parallel with the more common words. Together these other words are found a total of over 50 times. In particular, the very large proportion of the psalms of lament, whether individual or communal, make reference to enemies in one or more of these ways.

Who Are the Enemies?

Probably no topic has aroused more debate among students of the Psalms than the question of who these enemies are.[1] It may, of course, be argued that these words are not metaphors or poetic images, but should be taken literally. The enemies may be seen as real human beings of one kind or another. While we cannot deny that the original composer of a psalm may have had particular people in mind when he wrote of enemies, to limit the enemies to these people is to miss some of their real significance. Some commentators, especially those who identify the 'I' of the Psalms with the king, argue that the 'enemies' represent forces hostile to the king and the nation, either foreign armies or rebellious people within Israel itself.[2] Poems referring to enemies are then said either to have arisen out of particular situations of war or danger, or to be have been composed for use in rituals involving the king. This, however, ignores the fact that enemies are spoken of in a variety of different contexts, some of which appear to have nothing to do with war, and have no necessary connection with the king. Some talk about enemies occurs in psalms which appear to complain about illness: e.g. 6, 13, 38, 69. Wars, battles or armies are, in fact, very seldom mentioned in connection with enemies. There seems little justification for identifying the enemies totally with hostile foreign nations.

Others commentators maintain that the enemies in the 'I' psalms were accusers who brought false charges against an individual. Under Israelite law, a person who was accused of wrongdoing against someone else and who protested his innocence could take his case to the temple, where the priests would declare the judgement of Yhwh (Deut. 17:8ff). Some scholars believe that a number of the psalms (most notably 7 and 17, but possibly also 4, 5, 11, 23, 26, 57, 63 and maybe even others) were written for use by people seeking refuge in the temple in this way.[3] The 'enemies' in these psalms would then be the person's accusers. Such an interpretation may have historical validity in some cases, but it is hard to believe that it can be applied to a large number of psalms, or that it points us towards the real depth of meaning in the word 'enemies'.

More generally, many commentators and ordinary readers naturally assume that in the individual psalms the psalmists were referring to personal enemies, people of ill will who were troubling them in one way or another. In this case, we can understand them simply as any people who are hostile or who threaten or maltreat us. This is a more flexible approach, but it too causes difficulty. It is because the 'enemies' are understood as actual human beings, that they pose a problem for many Christian readers. When they find violent or vengeful feelings towards enemies, expressed sometimes in the context of otherwise profound and beautiful poems, (69:22–28; 139:19–22; 143:12), many people feel them to be incompatible with the injunction to 'love your enemies'. Because of this some modern versions of the Psalms deliberately bracket out the verses which express these sentiments. In one way or another, the verses which speak of enemies present us with problems if we understand them to refer literally to hostile human beings.

There is, however, another way of looking at the 'enemies'. Several things suggest that the psalmists have in mind something more mysterious and intangible than simply human or physical enemies. First we should note that words for 'enemies' are often used in poetic parallel or in close association with a variety of other images. Thus 'enemies' and 'mighty waters' can be spoken of together:

> He reached down from on high, he took me;
> he drew me out of mighty waters.
> He delivered me from my strong enemy,
> and from those who hated me. (18:16–17)

> Rescue me from sinking in the mire;
> let me be delivered from my enemies [literally, 'those who hate me']
> and from the deep waters. (69:14)

In Ps. 7 the enemies are spoken of as pursuers (vv. 1, 5), as wild beasts (v. 2), and as people who dig holes or pits as traps (v. 15). In Ps. 35 they are armed men who need to be repelled by spear and shield (vv. 1–3), people who lay hidden nets (v. 7), malicious witnesses who gather round and taunt (vv. 11, 15–16, 21), and lions who ravage (v. 17). In Ps. 59 they are people who lie in wait (v. 3), nations who plot treachery (v. 5), and wild dogs that howl about the city but with swords on their lips (vv. 6–7).

Ps. 124 provides a rich mixture of images, including enemies, beasts that devour, floods and raging waters and snares for trapping birds. Perhaps most significantly of all, the enemies are linked with death. In Ps. 6 they threaten to bring the psalmist down to Sheol (vv. 5, 10); in Ps. 40 they seek to snatch away his life by letting him sink in a miry bog (vv. 2, 14); and the imagery of the mighty waters referred to above also speaks of death, as we shall see. Altogether it is clear that the word 'enemy' has a wide semantic field. Its association with a variety of different images suggests that the enemies cannot be simply or entirely equated with certain human beings or hostile foreign nations, but may themselves be regarded as a poetic image which is capable of a wider and deeper meaning.

Secondly, we get a hint of this deeper meaning when we notice that in a number of places the enemies are said to be God's enemies.

> Even now your enemies are in tumult;
>> those who hate you have raised their heads. (83:2)

> Say to God, 'How awesome are your deeds!
>> Because of your great power, your enemies cringe before you.'
>> (66:3)

It is true that sometimes the 'enemies of God' appear to be Israel's aggressive neighbours, and that they may have been regarded as God's enemies simply because they were Israel's enemies. But equally, they may have been seen primarily as the enemies of God whose aggression towards Israel arose out of hostility to Israel's God, hostile powers who had 'set themselves in opposition to the creator and Lord of the peoples'.[4] Read either way, the word 'enemies' is taken onto a different plane. The hostility is not just animosity between human beings: it involved God himself. These 'enemies of God' are forces that operate beyond the human level. Ps. 68 tells of human battles but does so in the context of something more than human:

> O God when you went out before your people,
>> when you marched through the wilderness,
> the earth quaked, the heavens poured down rain
>> at the presence of God, the God of Sinai. (vv. 7–8)

This God is the 'rider in the heavens, the ancient heavens' (v. 33). So when the poem starts with the invitation to God:

> Let God rise up, let his enemies be scattered;
>> let all who hate him flee before him. (v. 1)

it envisages enemies not simply on the human but on the heavenly plane. Ps. 89 expresses this thought even more clearly. In verses which refer to ancient near eastern myth (and which we will return to later) it equates God's enemies with the forces of chaos which he overcame at creation:

> You rule the raging of the sea;
>> when its waves rise, you still them.
> You crushed Rahab like a carcass;
>> you scattered your enemies with your mighty arm. (vv. 9–10)

'Enemies' include superhuman forces which engage in battle with God.

Thirdly, a deeper meaning may also be implied by the use of the word 'enemy', in the singular, in a number of psalms:

> How long shall my enemy be exalted over me? (13:2)

> [You] have not delivered me into the hand of the enemy. (31:8)

> Why must I walk about mournfully
>> because the enemy oppresses me? (42:9)

> You are my refuge,
>> a strong tower against the enemy. (61:3)

> Hear my voice, O God, in my complaint;
>> preserve my life from the dread enemy [or 'dread of the
>>> enemy']. (64:1)

This use of the word in the singular may, of course, be no more than a stylistic device. The 'enemy' may be a collective word referring to the body of enemies as a whole[5] – a point supported by the fact that a plural word for enemies is sometimes used in the same psalm. But perhaps the use of the singular noun shows something more: that behind any human enemies there was a more mysterious and terrible enemy – the Enemy that inspired dread (64:1) The word 'dread' (*paḥad*) stands for a particular kind of awesome, paralysing fear, often of something more than human (2 Chr. 17:10; 20:29; Job 13:11), a panic or terror that falls on people mysteriously and suddenly (Job 4:14; 15:21; Isa. 24:18). The 'enemy' that inspires this dread may therefore be the evil force lying behind all 'enemies' –

possibly 'the archenemy himself, Death'.[6] That is not to say that the psalmists believed in a personal Devil – such a belief did not arise until later[7] – but a superhuman enemy of some sort is implied especially in the words of Ps. 8:

> You have founded a bulwark because of your foes,
> > to silence the enemy and the avenger. (v. 2)

Here, in the context of a poem about creation, the reference once again is apparently to ancient myth. The 'foes' and the 'enemy and the avenger' are the 'primeval opponents of Yhwh' at the time of creation.[8] It seems that the word 'enemy' retained connotations of transcendence, pointing to something beyond the human.

We conclude, then, that although the 'enemies' are usually spoken of as if they were human beings, and may indeed have had an original reference to particular people, there is also a deeper, symbolic reference to something superhuman. In describing human beings and their behaviour, the psalmists are saying something about a power which lies behind the people who are being spoken of. There is a metaphor here. If there is a literal reference there is also transferred reference, pointing to a deeper meaning. The 'enemies' may be human, but they stand for something beyond the human. And the characteristics attributed to the human enemies are also the characteristics of this hidden enemy.

An Image of Evil

What then are the characteristics of these enemies? To begin with we should note that the enemies the psalmists speak of were apparently not only hostile, but also wicked. The words 'enemies' and 'the wicked' are quite often found directly linked in poetic parallelism:

> You strike all my enemies on the cheek;
> > you break the teeth of the wicked. (3:7)

> . . . the wicked who despoil me,
> > my deadly enemies who surround me. (17:9)

> I am distraught by the noise of the enemy,
> > because of the clamour of the wicked. (55:2–3)

> Preserve my life from the dread enemy.
> > Hide me from the secret plots of the wicked. (64:1–2)

And there are a great many other places where the two ideas are closely associated with one another.[9] The enemies behave in wicked ways. They 'render evil for good' (38:20), 'boast of the abundance of their riches' (49:6), 'work evil' (59:2) and 'do not set God before them' (54:3); their 'hearts gather mischief' (41:6), they are 'insolent' and 'ruthless' (54:3) and 'bloodthirsty' (139:19). Elsewhere the enemies equated with the wicked are the enemies of God:

> The wicked perish,
>> and the enemies of the LORD are like the glory of the pastures;
>> they vanish – like smoke they vanish away. (37:20)

The enemies, then, are not only hostile and antagonistic; they are the godless, those who are opposed to the way of God.

Above all, the enemies are deceivers. Throughout the Psalter they are characterised by deceit and falsehood in a variety of forms. Again and again they are described as speaking lies, having lying lips, or uttering falsehood. They 'speak peace with their neighbours while mischief is in their hearts' (28:3); they speak 'with lying tongues' (109:2); their 'mouths speak lies', and their 'right hands are false' (144:8, 11). They 'accuse falsely' (69:4); 'utter empty words' (41:6); 'take pleasure in falsehood' (62:4); and 'love lying more than speaking the truth' (52:3). They 'have lying lips' (31:18) and 'speak lies' (5:6). They are 'pregnant with mischief and bring forth lies' (7:14). (See also 12:2; 109:20; 120:2, 3; 140:9, 11.)

These lies and falsehood are not purposeless gossip: they are uttered in the course of malicious schemes to bring harm or evil upon the victim. The enemies are people who conceive plots and scheme evil. 'They scheme together against me, as they plot to take my life'; (31:13) they 'devise evil against me' (35:4; see also: 7:14; 10:2; 21:11; 36:4; 59:5; 64:2, 4; 83:3; 140:2, 8). In pursuance of these underhand schemes they sometimes resort to flattery: 'they flatter with their tongues' (5:9); 'with flattering lips and a double heart they speak' (12:2); their speech is 'smoother than butter' (55:21). Sometimes it is a matter of whispering behind a person's back: 'All who hate me whisper together about me' (41:7); 'I hear the whispering of many' (31:13). Or they may lurk in hiding so as to catch their victim unawares: 'they lurk, they watch my steps' (56:6); 'they lie in wait for my life' (59:3); they 'watch for my life' (71:10); they 'shoot in the dark at the upright' (11:2). Ps. 10 gives us a particularly vivid description, which may be taken literally but which can also be read as a powerful poetic image:

Their mouths are filled with cursing and deceit and oppression;
  under their tongues are mischief and iniquity.
They sit in ambush in the villages;
  in hiding-places they murder the innocent.
Their eyes stealthily watch for the helpless;
  they lurk in secret like a lion in its covert;
they lurk that they may seize the poor;
  they seize the poor and drag them off in their net. (10:7–9)

The enemies, then, far from being armies on the field of battle, are usually hidden, secret foes who carry out their evil intentions by means of stealth, deceit and treachery. They are 'treacherous enemies' who 'conceive deceitful words' (35:19–20). They are 'cunning' (119:118). They have 'wicked and deceitful mouths' (109:2) and 'deceitful tongues' (120:2–3; 52:4). They are 'wantonly treacherous' (25:3); they 'meditate treachery all day long' (38:12) and 'treacherously plot evil' (59:5;. see also 5:6; 43:1; 50:19; 55:23). Their intention is not usually to attack people directly and openly, but to catch them unawares, to do them harm by trickery and stealth, to inflict evil on them in ways which they do not expect. They are an unseen, lurking malevolent danger. There is something sinister about them. 'Everything that these enemies do', says Kraus, 'is the result of such perverse and dark motivation that terror is the only possible response to these evil powers.'[10]

This sinister aspect is shown additionally by the link between 'enemies' and 'evildoers'.

Deliver me from my enemies, O my God . . .
  Deliver me from those who work evil. (59:1–2)

Preserve my life from the dread enemy . . .
  from the scheming of evildoers. (64:1–2)

For your enemies, O Lord,
  for your enemies shall perish;
  all evildoers shall be scattered. (92:9; see also 6:8)

The phrase 'evildoers', sometimes translated 'workers of iniquity', represents the Hebrew *pōʿᵃlê ʾāwen*, a phrase found 16 times in the Psalter (and only seven times in the rest of the Old Testament). The precise sense of the word *ʾāwen* ('evil' or 'iniquity') is disputed, but, as we saw in the previous chapter, it clearly carries some sinister overtones.[11] Mowinckel called it 'the operative evil power, pregnant with disaster and everything connected with it'; and claimed that the 'evil-doers' were 'people who by means of potent curses and other words and magic have brought upon a person impurity, weakness, illness or some other disaster'.[12] Not all scholars would go as far as that, but many would agree that there is something uncanny or even demonic about the *pō'ªlê 'āwen*. They are, in Eaton's words, 'sinister and malicious agencies'.[13] So when the enemies are linked with the evildoers they are shown to have a sinister, malevolent character.

By their activities the enemies may directly cause trouble and distress; but in addition they 'taunt' or 'mock' when things go wrong. The poet of Ps. 102 describes what seems like extreme bodily distress, and then adds;

> All day long my enemies taunt me;
>> those who deride me use my name for a curse. (v. 8)

Elsewhere the enemies 'scorn' the sufferers (109:25; 123:4), or taunt them with cries of 'Aha! aha!' (35:21; 40:15). The purpose of this taunting is not simply to cause distress. It is to undermine the faith and trust of those who are suffering, by persuading them that God has abandoned them. The adversaries say to the person in distress 'Where is your God?' (42:10). This underlines the real work and purpose of the enemies. Their intention is not primarily to cause suffering and distress, but through that distress to draw the sufferers away from God, to persuade them that God is no longer near and is unable to help.

It is probable that this imagery derives some of its power and its transcendent reference from its association with ancient near eastern mythology. In the 'enemy' of the psalmists there are echoes of the ancient myth in which at the creation of the world God overcame the power of primeval chaos. This was the original, the archetypal enemy, the opponent of God, of order and of goodness. 'The enemy powers are the floods of chaos which threaten the order of creation and strive to destroy it.'[14] This myth was probably not current any longer as a potent element in people's lives at the time when the Psalms were written. But as we saw in Chapter 3, the imagery associated with it would still have power to point to something transcendent. 'It cannot be overlooked that . . . in the Psalter there are tendencies towards transcendence that draw on the field of mythology.'[15] The 'enemy' may no longer have been the mythical creature slain by God, but the language of 'enemies' could still be used to evoke a sense of a mysterious power beyond human power, a 'primordial enmity overcome by Yhwh when he founded the world and established the firmament'.[16]

The psalmists, then, give us a picture of enemies who are wicked; who operate by stealth, lies and deceit, lurking in hidden places to catch people unawares; who can be equated with the malicious, sinister and rather mysterious 'evildoers'; who are the enemies – perhaps the Enemy – of God himself; and who try by taunting and mockery to draw their victims away from God. These enemies are thus an image of superhuman forces which are malevolent and insidious, hostile to both God and humans. They are a symbol of a hostile power which threatens people's lives from the outside. They have sometimes been described as 'demonic': they are 'demonic ministers of death',[17] or they have at least 'demonic overtones'[18] or 'almost demonic features'.[19] The Old Testament does not speak directly of demons, but in the image of the enemies there is a pointer to a power or powers which are external to human beings, and which operate mysteriously to do them harm in demonic fashion. There are 'hidden operations of malice which are too subtle and deep for the human defences of society'.[20]

But the power is not only external to humans. The image of the enemy is archetypal: it is a symbol of something embedded deeply in the human psyche. The enemies, says Eaton, 'have an archetypal character' which 'appears especially when they assume a sinister character'.[21] An archetypal image, as we have seen in Chapter 3, is one which connects with emotions buried deep in our unconscious. The image of the enemy speaks of something which has the power to affect us inwardly, to lure, to tempt and to deceive. In the words of a Jewish anthologist, it 'also refers to [the psalmist's] eyes, heart and desires which torment him with temptation to do evil'.[22] The poet's cry to God, says Davidson, 'suggests that these enemies are not actively persecuting the psalmist, but that he is fighting what is essentially an inner, spiritual battle'.[23] The enemies work within people, in subtle, insidious and hidden ways, through deception and falsehood, to draw them away from God.

Many people have raised the question of who are the 'enemies' in the psalms; and some, as we have seen, have identified them as the foreign nations. In fact, the enemies 'may have many identities'.[24] Whatever stands in opposition to God and seeks to assault the fundamentals of human life can be classified as an enemy. When the nations are referred to as enemies this does not tell us who the enemies are, but what the character of the nations is. By means of this image, the nations are being described as hostile to God.

The enemies, then, represent the opponents or adversaries of God, and they are a potent image of a power that operates mysteriously both in the affairs of the world and in human hearts to corrupt and spoil human life.

Faced with such an image we find ourselves using the word 'evil'. 'We cannot ignore,' says Lindström, 'the demonic color and the characteristics of superhuman evil that are used in the descriptions of the enemy.'[25] The enemies are, in Kraus's words, 'the "primal image" of all that is evil, all that ruins human beings, all that corrupts creation, and all that separates from [God]'.[26] Whatever the original psalmists may have had in mind at the physical and literal level, at the level of image and symbolism, the enemies represent, as Ricoeur says, 'the forces of evil in our history'.[27]

Wild Beasts

The two other sets of images in this cluster are used in connection with the enemies and are often applied to them. They fill out the picture of what the enemies are like, and what it feels like to be attacked by them. The first of these, images of wild beasts, are less common than those of the enemies, but much more graphic. Three kinds of threatening and dangerous animals are mentioned in the Psalter. First, there are the *lions*. Three Hebrew words translated 'lion' or 'young lion' are used a total of nine times to describe danger or threat, usually the danger presented by enemies or the wicked.

The lions have two main characteristics. First, they are immensely ferocious, and tear and devour their prey with their mouths and teeth.

> They [the enemies] are like a lion eager to tear. (17:12)

> They open their mouths wide at me,
>   like a ravening and roaring lion. (22:13)

> I lie down among lions
>   that greedily devour human prey;
> their teeth are spears and arrows,
>   their tongues sharp swords. (57:4)

Secondly, lions are especially dangerous because they lurk in secret, and spring out unexpectedly:

> They [the wicked] lurk in secret like a lion in its covert. (10:9)

> [They are] like a young lion lurking in ambush. (17:12)

Because of this God is urged to rescue the psalmist from this ferocious beast:

Save me from all my pursuers, and deliver me,
  or like a lion they will tear me apart. (7:1–2)

Save me from the mouth of the lion! (22:21)

O God, break the teeth in their mouths;
  Tear out the fangs of the young lions, O LORD! (58:6)

Lions were, of course, real beasts which were to be found in the Palestine of that time, but they represent something more than actual wild animals. That they are a broad metaphor standing for terrible danger of various kinds can be seen especially in Ps. 57:4 (above), where they are associated with spears, arrows, swords and fire. The second line of this verse says literally 'they are aflame for the sons of man', using a verb 'closely associated with destructive fire (cf. 83:14; 97:3)'.[28] Moreover, they also represent a supernatural danger, since 'from the most ancient times demons have been portrayed as lions'.[29]

The danger represented by *wild bulls* is mentioned only infrequently in the Psalms but the image is a vivid one. The most significant reference is in Ps. 22, a poem in which the poet uses a great variety of metaphors to describe his distress.[30] The words,

Many bulls encircle me,
  strong bulls of Bashan surround me. (v. 12)

are one way of expressing a sense of terrible danger. Bulls were large, strong and fierce, their strength and ferocity being emphasised by their horns which were particularly dangerous. The wild ones roamed in open country, and could be a symbol of uncontrollability as well as strength, as in Job 39:9–12. It was perhaps for this reason that they were felt to have a mysterious and awesome quality, and were widely used as religious symbols in near-eastern cults. Possibly this quality lies behind the use in 22:21 of another word, *rēmîm* whose meaning is not certain but which is usually translated 'wild oxen'. The translation 'unicorns', which is preserved in the King James Version, (and which seems to have arisen by deriving the word *rēmîm* from the Hebrew word *rām*, meaning 'raised up' or 'high', which was taken to refer to the creatures' horns),[31] possibly also conveys something of the sense of mystery surrounding these strange beasts. It is not surprising, then, that wild bulls were also used in the near east as a symbol for demons,[32] and therefore that the words in Ps. 22:12 should be read as a metaphor not for people but for demonic powers.[33]

Thirdly there are the *dogs*. These were no friendly pets, but untamed creatures which roamed in packs around the outskirts of human settlements. They did not seize and tear their prey apart like lions, nor threaten with their power and strength like bulls. Rather, they were scavengers that snarled and growled in anger as they prowled around people's houses by night. They devoured anything, even human corpses (1 Kings 21:23; 2 Kings 9:36). Twice in the Psalms the enemies or evildoers are compared to these dogs.

> Each evening they come back,
>   howling like dogs
>   and prowling about the city. (59:6, 14)

> For dogs are all around me;
>   a company of evildoers encircles me. (22:16)

And so, once again, the psalmist calls to God for deliverance:

> Deliver my soul from the sword,
>   my life from the power of the dog! (22:20)

The fact that they roamed in packs made them a suitable image for 'gangs of evildoers'. Their habit of scavenging among the refuse made them dirty, unsavoury, dangerous and horrible, 'waiting to be at the death of the psalmist'.[34] 'The half-wild pariah dogs', says Keel,

> were undoubtedly possessed of greater affinity with dangerous
> demons than with triumphant rulers . . . If in any psalm the
> adversaries of the suppliant bear demonic features it is in Ps. 59
> where they are twice compared with pariah dogs.[35]

The image of the wild beasts, therefore, is significant in two ways. First, it is widely agreed that it refers not simply to certain hostile human beings but to some kind of evil power. The wild beasts are 'demonic, beast-like powers';[36] 'demonic powers that separate [the psalmist] from God;[37] 'forces which seek to thwart the purpose of God to sustain his order';[38] 'powers that threaten the life of God's people'.[39] If they are not actual demons, they are at least 'reflections on the helpless fear which overwhelms [the psalmist]'.[40]

Secondly, the danger to human beings is of a particularly life-threatening kind. The beasts are 'cruel death powers'.[41] The enemies they represent 'come to devour my flesh' (27:2), to 'eat up my people as they eat bread' (14:4). One of their special characteristics is that 'they do not want the complainant's goods and chattels; they do not want to rob him of office or of some other quantity; they seek his life and that alone.'[42] The image of the wild beasts points to some power or powers which are particularly nasty, dangerous and evil.

Nets, Snares, Traps and Pits

The third set of images, referring to devices used by hunters to catch animals and birds, also tells us something about the enemies. A number of different Hebrew words are involved, which sometimes overlap in meaning; and the words used to translate them are often interchangeable. But there are slight differences in meaning, which draw our attention to different characteristics of the enemies.

Among these devices was the *rešet*, or net, used for catching all kinds of creatures and things. Sometimes it was spread high up on poles to catch birds; sometimes just above the ground so that an animal's foot would get caught in it. There was also the *paḥ*, or trap, mainly for catching birds, sometimes referred to as the 'snare of the fowler'. The *môqēš*, usually translated snare, refers more especially to the bait or lure used to entice a creature into a trap. And finally there is the *šaḥat*, or pit. This word is used, along with others of similar meaning, to refer to pits of different kinds, as we shall see later; but in this context it means a 'deliberately dug pit-fall',[43] a disguised or camouflaged hole into which unwary creatures could fall. It could even be used for catching a lion (Ezek. 19:4, 8).

All of these are applied figuratively to enemies, often in parallel with one another.

> The arrogant have hidden a trap for me,
>> and with cords they have spread a net;
>> along the road they have set snares for me. (140:5)

> For without cause they hid their net for me;
>> without cause they dug a pit for my life. (35:7)

> They set a net for my steps;
>> my soul was bowed down.
> They dug a pit in my path. (57:6)

> Keep me from the trap that they have laid for me,
>> and from the snares of evildoers. (141:9)

The various words involved, and their different nuances, point to a number of different characteristics of the enemies. The first is something we have met already, the hidden, unexpected nature of the danger. The trapping devices work by being concealed, so that they can catch the unsuspecting creature unawares. This is seen as part of the strategy of the enemies: they are described as deliberately hiding traps or snares or nets (9:15; 31:4; 35:8; 140:5; 142:3). By concealing their devices, the adversaries 'spread uncertainty, anxiety and sudden inescapable disaster'.[44] As we have seen in connection with other images, the enemy works by stealth, cunning and deceit.

Secondly, the use of the word *môqēš*, or snare, draws attention to the fact that the enemies, in addition to spreading uncertainty, can also lure and entice their victims. The word is 'figurative of what allures and entraps anyone to disaster or ruin'.[45] So idol worship can be a dangerous enticement:

> They served their idols,
> which became a snare to them. (106:36)

– a thought expressed by the use of this word in various parts of the Old Testament (Exod. 23:33; Deut. 7:16; Judg. 2:3; 8:27). The *môqēš* stands for 'something which attracts and then destroys the unsuspecting victim'.[46] This is an aspect of the enemy's cunning and deceit.

Thirdly, the words together present an image of being caught, trapped and bound. The net spread just above the ground is something in which, figuratively, our foot can be caught, so that we are held captive, and in need of God's rescuing:

> He will pluck my feet out of the net. (25:15)

> In the net that they hid has their own foot been caught. (9:15)

The net can not only trip and entangle us, it can also hold us prisoner. The image of being imprisoned is one we will encounter again, but here already we have the sense that we can be bound and restricted. The enemy can take people captive. The image of the net can express 'the experience of the anxiety and despair of a human being who feels caught, trapped, hemmed in'.[47]

All of this adds to the sense that at one level, these images refer to evil. The snare has become a common image for evil, the phrase 'snare of the devil' being found in the New Testament (1 Tim. 3:7; 2 Tim. 2:26), and also, for example, in the well-known words attributed to St Anthony of the

Desert: 'I saw the snares that the enemy spreads out over the world'.[48] The sense that this imagery speaks of evil is reinforced by the repeated statement in the Psalms that the enemies who prepare these traps, snares or pits will be caught in them themselves:

> They make a pit, digging it out,
>> and fall into the hole that they have made. (7:15)

> And let the net that they hid ensnare them;
>> let them fall in it – to their ruin. (35:8)

> They dug a pit in my path,
>> but they have fallen into it themselves. (57:6)

> Let the wicked fall into their own nets,
>> while I alone escape. (141:10; see also 9:15, quoted above)

This thought arises not simply from a desire for justice or vengeance, but from a conviction that those who engage in evil will find themselves trapped in it; that evil brings its own nemesis. The trap which ensnares the trapper is a vivid image of this. Evil is a snare, into which the susceptible are enticed, and in which the unwary are caught and held, but in which the evildoer is also trapped.

We have, then, in this first cluster these three sets of images which can be read as speaking of evil. They were apparently evoked by the situations of distress in which the psalmists found themselves, and may originally have described some of the causes of the distress. But they point beyond the literal reference to something transcendent – a hostile power which is at enmity with God, which operates in treacherous, deceitful and malevolent ways, both externally in the community and internally in people's hearts; a power which is like a ferocious and powerful beast, lurking to seize and kill, or a hidden trap or net threatening to ensnare and imprison. This, however, is only one part of the picture of evil which we find in the Psalms. For a fuller understanding we need to look at the other clusters of images.

Chapter 6

Images of Distress: (2) Being Overwhelmed

Cisterns

The images in the second cluster have to do with the feeling of sinking or being overwhelmed. We start with a little image found only a couple of times, that of a water cistern. These were common in the dry countries of the near east in biblical times, and consisted of large holes dug in the ground, and lined with waterproof lime plaster, so that they filled up with water when it rained.[1] At times the water could drain away or be used up, leaving only a deposit of mud in the bottom of the cistern. When Ps. 40 speaks of a *bôr* or 'pit' it apparently refers to a cistern of this kind:

> He drew me up from the desolate pit,
>   out of the miry bog. (v. 2)

The same thing seems to provide some of the background for Ps. 69 although, as we shall see, other imagery is also present:

> I sink in deep mire,
>   where there is no foothold. (v. 2)

> With your faithful help rescue me
>   from sinking in the mire. (vv. 13–14)

Here there is no explicit reference to a cistern or pit, but the same word for mud or mire is used as in Ps. 40, and the thought of sinking in the mud suggests the same image.

Such pits were apparently sometimes used as places of imprisonment (Exod. 12:29; Isa. 24:22; Zech. 9:11; Lam. 3:53, 55); and the metaphor in these psalms is especially reinforced by two well-known Old

Testament passages where a person is 'thrown' into an empty pit or cistern. Joseph's brothers 'took him and threw him into a pit (*bôr*). The pit
was empty; there was no water in it' (Gen. 37:24). And similarly Jeremiah
was thrown into a cistern (*bôr*): 'there was no water in the cistern, but
only mud, and Jeremiah sank in the mud' (Jer. 38:6). The link between
these stories and these two psalms is strengthened by the use of the same
Hebrew words for cistern, for mud and for sinking. It has been suggested
that the poet of the psalms had actually been thrown into one himself; or
even that the poet of Ps. 69 was Jeremiah himself,[2] but to read these
psalm passages literally in this way is surely to misunderstand their poetic
imagery. The psalmist is using a graphic and powerful metaphor to
describe extreme distress, which is likened to the feeling of sinking into
deep mud where there is no bottom and 'no foothold'. The pit is 'desolate' (Ps. 40:2), literally a 'pit of roaring', a word which is sometimes
taken to mean 'tumultuous', but which may perhaps suggest the cries of
a person sinking helplessly into the mud. There is a sense of panic, of
being overwhelmed, of going down without anything to hold on to or
stand on. What is needed is a foothold (69:2), or someone to set one's feet
upon a rock and make one's steps secure (40:2).

The Mighty Waters

The metaphor of the cistern, however, itself gets somewhat overwhelmed
and entwined in the larger and complex image of the waters and floods.
In Ps. 69 the words 'I sink in deep mire' are accompanied by 'the waters
have come up to my neck', and 'I have come into deep waters, and the
flood sweeps over me'. The Psalms use a great many words to refer to the
threat of being overwhelmed by water: waters, floods, torrents, waves,
breakers, billows, cataracts, the sea, the deep or depths. Sometimes they
express an individual person's distress:

> All your waves and your billows have gone over me. (42:7)

> Your dread assaults destroy me,
>   They surround me like a flood all day long. (88:16–17)

> Therefore let all who are faithful
>   offer prayer to you;
> at a time of distress, the rush of mighty waters
>   shall not reach them. (32:6; see also 18:16; 69:15; 88:7)

In other places they refer to danger threatening the community or nation:

Therefore we will not fear, though the earth should change,
  though the mountains shake in the heart of the sea;
though its waters roar and foam. (46:2–3)

Then the flood would have swept us away,
  the torrent would have gone over us;
then over us would have gone
  the raging waters. (124:4–5)

Now it may be thought that the waters or waves are just a graphic way of describing the experience of being overwhelmed by distress or disaster, and that the image is simply one of the physical danger posed by deep or rushing water. The picture of the 'rush of mighty waters' of Ps. 32:6 'may simply be that of a flash flood pouring down a wadi';[3] or the use of the sea as a metaphor may arise from 'the powerful impression which its surging waves make'.[4] To understand the waters in this way, however, is to miss much of the richness of meaning in the metaphor; because this image, perhaps more than any other, refers back to and draws its emotional power from ancient near eastern myth.

Canaanite Myth

It is now generally recognised that the myths which underlie the mythical terminology of the Old Testament were principally those of the Canaanites, who were the near neighbours and the cultural predecessors of the Israelites.[5] Their creation myth told of how the gods were threatened by Yamm (meaning 'Sea'), the seven-headed monster of the sea.[6] His other name Nahar, meaning 'River', shows that he represents not simply the sea but the threat posed by water generally; the threat of watery chaos. Yamm thus stands for primeval chaos, the power which opposed or prevented the creation of an orderly world. In the myth he demands that his lordship be acknowledged. The champion who arose to combat Yamm was Baal, the god of storms, rain and fertility. Supplied with two marvellous clubs by Kothar, the craftsman god, Baal does battle with Yamm and overcomes him. Yamm is apparently killed, and yet it seems that he does not die, but is only confined to his proper sphere,[7] since he appears again in the story. In another development, Baal does battle with the earth monster Mot, or Death, and is apparently killed by him, but is subsequently brought to life again by his sister or consort Anat, who defeats Mot and slays him. There is also a variant of the Yamm myth, in which Baal and Anat kill the sea dragon Lotan, a name paralleled in the biblical 'Leviathan'. On the instructions of 'El, the high god, Kothar builds a magnificent palace for Baal, who now rules supreme over the earth, and whose power is seen in the storms. It is Baal who brings rain and fertility to the earth.

We have seen in Chapter 3 that imagery based on myths can persist in a language and culture even when the myths themselves no longer have explanatory or earth-renewing power, and this is true of these stories of Yamm and Baal. Canaanite poems about the lordship of Baal, the storm god, are very close to the surface of some of the psalms, particularly Pss 29 and 93, and the mythology also underlies some of the imagery of waters. This can be seen initially from the use in the Psalms of the phrase 'many waters' or 'great waters' (18:16; 29:3; 32:6; 77:19; 93:4; 107:23; 144:7), the Hebrew *mayim rabbîm* reflecting the Canaanite 'Rabbim', one of the titles of the sea monster.[8] The 'many waters' either refer to or have an echo of the primeval waters of chaos. For although the psalmists did not hold to a myth of the overcoming of the sea in the same way as the Canaanites did, they did believe that at the creation of the universe Yhwh had overcome the power of chaos, and this power could be represented, not only by the image of the waters or the sea generally, but also by that of a sea monster or dragon of different names. Thus Ps. 74, describing the work of creation, speaks not only of the sea (Hebrew *yām*), but of dragons (*tannînîm*) and the sea monster Leviathan:

> You divided the sea by your might;
> > you broke the heads of the dragons in the waters.
> You crushed the heads of Leviathan;
> > you gave him as food for the creatures of the wilderness.
> You cut openings for springs and torrents;
> > you dried up ever-flowing streams [*naharôt*, cf 'Nahar' mentioned
> > above]. (vv. 13–15)

Here Leviathan is said to have been crushed, and his body dispersed. By contrast Ps. 104, a psalm of creation, suggests that Leviathan was tamed and made into a plaything:

> Yonder is the sea, great and wide,
> > creeping things innumerable are there,
> > living things both small and great.
> There go the ships,
> > and Leviathan that you formed to sport in it. (vv. 25–26; see also
> > Job 41:1; Isa. 27:1)

Elsewhere the dragon of the sea is referred to as Rahab:

> You rule the raging of the sea;
>> when its waves rise, you still them.
> You crushed Rahab like a carcass;
>> you scattered your enemies with your mighty arm. (89:9–10; see
>> Job 9:13; 26:12; Isa. 51:9)

Leviathan, as we have seen, is the Hebrew name for the creature referred to by the Canaanites as Lotan; but Rahab is found only in the Israelite tradition. It is probable that Leviathan and Rahab were alternative names for the same creature.[9] The word *tannîn* is a not a proper name but a general word for a monster or dragon (Gen. 1:21; Ps. 148:7), but its use in parallel with Leviathan or Rahab in Ps. 74:13 (quoted above), as well as in Isa. 27:1; 51:9, shows that it too can refer specifically to the sea monster destroyed by Yhwh at the time of creation.[10] Similarly the general word *yām* usually simply means 'sea', but it is also used in some of these verses in parallel with the named sea monsters (89:9–10; 74:13; Isa. 51:9–10). There were thus many ways of referring to the dragon of the waters.

These myth-based images of the sea with its dragons and monsters expressed the belief that in creating the world God overcame primeval chaos, which was like 'great waters' or an untameable sea. Chaos was a power hostile to God, like the sea dragon in the myth, a dangerous force which threatened God himself. This primordial chaos was evil, because it stood in opposition to God, and it had to be overcome if God was to bring about his purpose for the world. The dragon had to be slain. The mythical language of the Psalms celebrates the slaying of the dragon and the overcoming of evil in the form of primeval chaos.

These mythological concepts of a divine victory underlie a great many of the references to the waters and the seas in the Psalms. Since it was this victory that led to the separation of the dry land from the waters, the idea of God's triumph over the dragon and the waters of primeval chaos is implicit when this separation is spoken of.

> He gathered the waters of the sea as in a bottle;
>> he put the deeps in storehouses. (33:7)

> The earth is the Lord's and all that is in it,
>> the world and those who live in it;
> for he has founded it on the seas,
>> and established it on the rivers. (24:1–2)

> The waters stood above the mountains.
>> At your rebuke they flee. (104:6–7)

According to this view, creation was accomplished when God divided the sea by his might (74:13), and 'spread out the earth on the waters' (136:6). Out of the primeval waters of chaos the land emerged.

Historicising the Myth

But this mythological concept of God's victory over primeval chaos was put to another use in the Old Testament. The myth of the sea dragon was re-interpreted by some writers, so that it referred not only to creation but to events in Israel's history, in particular the Exodus from Egypt. The ancient creation myth was historicised, and Rahab, the mythical sea monster, could now be used as a name for Egypt (Ps. 87:4; Isa. 30:7). Just how this came about is not clear, but as Anderson suggests, '[t]he reason for this extension of usage may have been the belief that in some way Egypt was part of the hostile primeval Chaos.'[11] So Deutero-Isaiah, in a passage we have referred to already, after recalling how God 'cut Rahab in pieces', and 'pierced the dragon', relates this to God's victory over the Red Sea at the Exodus:

> Was it not you who dried up the sea,
>> the waters of the great deep;
> who made the depths of the sea a way
>> for the redeemed to cross over? (Isa. 51:10)

Some of the psalmists also clearly link God's overcoming of the waters at creation with the Exodus and God's holding back of the waters of the Red Sea.

> When the waters saw you, O God,
>> when the waters saw you, they were afraid;
>> the very deep trembled.
> Your way was through the sea,
>> your path, through the mighty waters [*mayim rabbîm*];
>> yet your footprints were unseen.
> You led your people like a flock
>> by the hand of Moses and Aaron. (77:16, 19, 20)

These verses can be read as having a double reference. While explicitly telling of God's action at the Red Sea they have an echo of his victory over the waters of primordial chaos. It is noticeable that when the psalmists tell of the Israelites' escape from Egypt at the Exodus, they seldom refer to the overcoming of the Egyptian forces. Even in Pss 106:10–11 and 136:15, where there is reference to the opposing army, the emphasis is, as elsewhere, more on the dividing of the sea than on the victory over the armies of Pharaoh. This is surely because victory over the sea carried powerful emotional and symbolic meaning, since it recalled Yhwh's original victory over the waters of chaos. Thus even when there is no explicit reference to the myth of creation, or to the overcoming of primeval chaos, the thought of this original victory must lie behind the many references to the waters at the Exodus. The idea of dividing the sea, in particular, is used both of the creation (74:13) and of the Exodus:

> He divided the sea and let them pass through it,
>   and made the waters stand like a heap. (78:13)

> He turned the sea into dry land;
>   they passed through the river [*nāhār*] on foot. (66:6)

> The waters covered their adversaries;
>   not one of them was left. (106:11)

> [He] divided the Red Sea in two . . .
>   and made Israel pass through the midst of it. (136:13–14)

> When Israel went out from Egypt . . .
> The sea looked and fled;
>   Jordan turned back. (114:1, 3)

In view of the symbolic significance of the waters, when Yhwh rescued his people from Egypt he was felt to be delivering them not only from the army of Pharaoh which was pursuing them, but from the forces of evil. Egypt, as we have seen, was identified with Rahab, the mythical dragon and symbol of evil. At the Exodus God repeated his original victory, and he did so by reasserting his power over the sea.

For the Israelites, therefore, God's victory over the waters was not only a mythical way of describing the act of creation sometime in the past, but was something which was repeated in the life of his people. The myth was historicised, and later events were understood in the light of it. If it applied to the Exodus, it could be applied to the exile in Babylon as well. To some people at the time of the exile, '[i]t appeared that the powers of chaos, defeated at creation and in the Exodus, had reasserted themselves, but, as on the earlier occasions, they were to be overcome again.'[12] So the poet of Deutero-Isaiah who, as we saw above, describes the Exodus in terms of the ancient myth (Isa. 51:9–10, quoted above) sees this as a sign of the way that God will act again to bring his people out of exile in Babylon, for he adds in the next verse:

> So the ransomed of the LORD shall return,
>   and come to Zion with singing. (v. 11)

That is to say, God's power over the waters continues. His victory over the sea was an act which took place at the time of creation in the past, but he still has sovereignty over the chaotic waters. The psalmists move easily between past and present, assisted by the fact that Hebrew verbs do not necessarily carry specific time reference. Thus Ps. 65 'moves from the thought of Yhwh's victory over the chaos waters at creation to the idea of his victory over the powers of chaos embodied in the enemy nations in the present':[13]

> By your strength you established the mountains;
>   you are girded with might.
> You silence the roaring of the seas,
>   the roaring of their waves,
>   the tumult of the peoples. (vv. 6–7)

Indeed, it is often difficult to know whether the psalmists are speaking of God's original act in creation, or of his present and continuing sovereignty.

> You rule the raging of the sea;
>   when its waves rise, you still them. (89:9)

> The voice of the LORD is over the waters;
>   the God of glory thunders,
>   the LORD, over mighty waters [*mayim rabbîm*]. (29:3)

> The floods have lifted up, O LORD,
>   the floods have lifted up their voice;
>   the floods lift up their roaring.
> More majestic than the thunders of mighty waters, [*mayim rabbîm*]
>   more majestic than the waves of the sea,
>   majestic on high is the LORD! (93:3–4)

The myth of God's victory over primeval chaos was thus used as a way of affirming trust in his continuing power to protect in times of danger.

Since he has overcome the waters of chaos, he still has power to restrain and control them. Those who trust in him can therefore have confidence that he will preserve them and keep them safe, even when the waters threaten:

> God is our refuge and strength,
>> a very present help in trouble.
> Therefore we will not fear, though the earth should change,
>> though the mountains shake in the heart of the sea;
> though its waters roar and foam,
>> though the mountains tremble with its tumult. (46:1–3)

The image of the waters became part of the liturgy, through which the people sang of their trust in the sovereignty of God over the powers of evil.

Continued Threat

But there is another side to this. If God had to continue to assert his power over the waters there must have been a contrary power which God still needed to keep in control. The forces of chaos were not totally destroyed, but were still active and needed to be held in check. According to the cosmology of the time, the earth was still surrounded on all sides – below, above and at its circumference – by the waters of chaos, which God had controlled and divided at the time of creation, but which still threatened to rush in and overwhelm the created world. So the psalmists assert two apparently contradictory things. On the one hand they celebrate the fact that God has overcome the dragon of the deep, crushed the heads of Leviathan, and subdued the unruly waters. That is to say, he has already won the victory over primeval chaos, and defeated the power of evil. On the other hand, they make it clear that the waters are still resurgent, the powers of chaos and evil still pose a threat to human life and the good order of the world, so that God needs constantly to reassert his power and subdue them afresh. Jon Levenson, in his important book *Creation and the Persistence of Evil*, argues that in the Old Testament the creation of the world did not bring to an end the power of chaos and evil. On the contrary, in some texts (Ps. 104:6–9; Job 38:8–11) 'we have a sense of the Sea as a somewhat sinister force that, left to its own, would submerge the world and forestall the ordered reality we call creation.' He maintains that

> the confinement of chaos rather than its elimination is the essence of creation, and the survival of ordered reality hangs upon God's

vigilance in ensuring that those cosmic dikes do not fall, that the bars and doors of the Sea's jail cell do not give way, that the great fish does not slip its hook.

Levenson points out that even those passages which seem to speak of God having destroyed the sea monster (Ps. 74:12–17; Isa. 51:9–11, see above) are set amongst verses which make it clear that God has not finally got rid of evil, and that the powers of chaos are still rampant.[14]

Levenson is not alone in recognising this continuing threat of chaos. The medieval Jewish scholar Rabbi David Kimchi ('Radak'), commenting on Ps. 89:9, ('You rule the raging of the sea'), maintained that 'the sea waters would tower over the land and flood the earth if God did not rule the waters and confine them within their boundaries.'[15] Other modern scholars make the same point. Robert Davidson speaks of 'forces of chaos [which were] conquered in creation but which ever threaten to break into the ordered universe';[16] and H. G. May, in a study of the 'many waters' in the Old Testament, regards them not only as 'intransigent elements which had to be quelled by Yhwh before creation could begin', but as forces which 'must ever be defeated by him as he continues his activity in history'.[17] There is thus a 'recurrent threat of Chaos'.[18] Leviathan is 'a symbol of evil which can render human lives chaotic even now'.[19] By using the language of myth and the great monster the Old Testament 'clearly acknowledged evil's continuing strength and power.'[20] Indeed, it may be said that the Old Testament acknowledges a dualism in the cosmos.[21] The power of Yhwh is supreme, but alongside it there is a rival power which has indeed been overcome by God's act in ordering the world, but which has persisted throughout human history, constantly threatening to bring about disorder and evil.

The people of Israel, of course, knew this in their own experience. Although in their liturgy they celebrated God's victory over the dragon of the deep and his continuing sovereignty over the powers of evil and chaos, this power and victory of God were not always obvious. Dangers and disasters still threatened the people of God. Life-denying forces of evil and wickedness still laid waste to human life. The earth still had its dark places which were full of the haunts of violence. What the psalmists affirmed about God's power over the waters of chaos seemed to be denied by their own experience of the world about them. There was what Levenson has called a 'yawning gap between the liturgical affirmation of God's absolute sovereignty and the empirical reality of evil triumphant and unchecked'.[22] If God had power over the forces of chaos he did not seem to exert it. If he was in control, why did he allow hostile powers to play havoc with people's lives? It was this strange contradiction which led the psalmists to cry out to God to assert himself. God was clearly not powerless in face of evil forces – by reason of his victory he had the supreme authority – but for some reason he was not exerting that authority or exercising that power. So he had to be called upon to arise and act. Psalm 74, in telling of God's victory over Leviathan and the 'dragons in the waters' (vv. 13–14, see above), encloses this statement of faith within complaints that he is doing nothing, and pleas for him to act:

> How long, O God, is the foe to scoff?
>> Is the enemy to revile your name for ever?
> Why do you hold back your hand;
>> why do you keep your hand in your bosom? (74:10–11)

> Remember this, O LORD, how the enemy scoffs,
>> and an impious people reviles your name.
> Have regard for your covenant,
>> for the dark places of the land are full of the haunts of violence.
>> (74:18, 20)

Similarly Psalm 89, which celebrates God's rule over the raging of the sea and his crushing of the monster Rahab (vv. 9–10, see above), goes on to lament God's present inertia, 'How long, O LORD? Will you hide yourself for ever? . . . Lord, where is your steadfast love of old?' (vv. 46, 49). The dread forces of evil have been overcome, but they still endanger ordered human life. The waters of chaos still surge around, threatening to sweep over and overwhelm the lives both of nations and of individual people.

This then leads us to a deeper understanding of the imagery of the waters in the Psalms. We saw at the start of this chapter that the image of the deep waters is used in the psalms of complaint to express the sense of being overwhelmed by distress of one kind or another: 'The waters have come up to my neck', 'I sink in deep waters'. These psalms speak of 'a rush of mighty waters', of 'waves and billows' or of being surrounded 'like a flood'. We can now see that this image is not just a simple metaphor for a feeling of being overwhelmed by troubles, because behind it there lies the emotional power of the ancient myth of God's victory over the waters of chaos and primeval evil. As we saw in Chapter 3, myth-based images can continue to carry emotional power even after the myth is no longer in active use, and point to something transcendent and superhuman. So in these psalms the image of the waters speaks not only of ordinary human troubles, but of the threat of something greater and more sinister, the fear of being engulfed by the dark power of evil in the form of chaos. The plea for rescue from the waves was a plea for deliverance from evil. This may be seen in psalms of other types also. In some the image of the waters is combined with the image of the enemies, which, as we have seen, points beyond human enemies to the mysterious, lurking power of evil.

> Stretch out your hand from on high;
>> set me free and rescue me from the mighty waters [*mayim rab-bîm*], from the hand of aliens,
> whose mouths speak lies,
>> and whose right hands are false. (144:7–8)

> He reached down from on high, he took me;
>> he drew me out of mighty waters [*mayim rabbîm*],
> He delivered me from my strong enemy,
>> and from those who hated me. (18:16–17)

And even the story, in Ps. 107, of those who 'went down to the sea in ships' can be read as more than a description of danger at sea. Its account of how some who did 'business on the mighty waters (*mayim rabbîm*)' found themselves in extreme danger from the stormy waves, takes on a deeper meaning when we remember the symbolic significance of the 'mighty waters':

> Then they cried to the LORD in their trouble,
>> and he brought them out from their distress;
> he made the storm be still,
>> and the waves of the sea were hushed. (vv. 28–29)

Here and throughout the Psalter, the imagery of the sea, of the mighty waters, of waves, billows, floods and torrents, like the imagery of enemies, speaks not only of human distress but of the still present threat from the forces of primeval chaos and superhuman evil, and of the need to 'cry to the LORD' who overcame them at the time of creation and who alone can control and subdue them now.

The Great Deep
The Hebrew word *t^ehôm* meaning 'the deep' or 'depths', adds a further dimension to this imagery. This is a word which has an air of mystery

about it. It occurs at the start of the creation story in the first chapter of
Genesis – 'and darkness covered the face of the deep [*tᵉhôm*]' (Gen. 1:2)
– where it represents the mysterious uncreated chaos which was a 'formless void' (*tōhû wābōhû*). It occurs too in some of the psalms which
describe creation. In broad terms it can be taken, like the other words, to
refer to the 'mighty waters', the waters of chaos which God overcame by
the act of creation, although we are sometimes left uncertain whether the
tᵉhôm was created by God, or whether it refers to pre-existent waters
which God separated or divided as he created the world:

> He gathered the waters of the sea as in a bottle;
>   he put the deeps [*tᵉhôm*] in storehouses. (33:7)

> You set the earth on its foundations,
>   so that it shall never be shaken.
> You cover it with the deep [*tᵉhôm*] as with a garment;
>   the waters stood above the mountains. (104:5–6)

> Praise the LORD from the earth,
>   you sea monsters and all deeps [*tᵉhōmôt*, pl]. (148:7)

In this last verse, *tᵉhôm* is used in parallel with 'sea monsters' (*tannînîm*).
There is no suggestion that *tᵉhôm* was the name of a monster or dragon of
the deep; but the fact that it is never used with the article, and that it can
be referred to as 'the deep that couches beneath' (Gen. 49:25; Deut.
33:13, RSV) suggests that the word 'retains the flavour of myth' and has
the 'possibility of personality'.[23] Like other associated words, *tᵉhôm*
points to the mysterious power of chaos. And as with other words for the
primordial waters, its meaning could be extended so that it referred not
only to the creation but to God's act of dividing the waters of the Red Sea
at the time of the Exodus from Egypt:

> When the waters saw you, O God,
>   when the waters saw you, they were afraid;
>   the very deep [*tᵉhōmôt*] trembled. (77:16)

> He rebuked the Red Sea, and it became dry;
>   he led them through the deep [*tᵉhōmôt*] as through a desert. (106:9)

But *tᵉhôm* has an additional aspect: it seems always to carry the sense
of something unfathomable. It means the bottomless ocean, the depths
which have no limit. It is mysterious, it cannot be known or contained,

and it is also dangerous. It is both bottomless and boundless; one cannot reach its end or touch ground beneath it. If one sinks in these depths one is lost, for there is nothing beneath one's feet. So *tᵉhôm*, while it is, like the 'many waters', an image of primeval chaos, is also used as an image of deep personal distress, of being in the depths of despair, or out of one's depth in misery. The psalmist of Ps. 71 feels himself to have been sunk in the *tᵉhôm*, the bottomless subterranean waters.

> You who have made me see many troubles and calamities
> > will revive me again;
> from the depths [*tᵉhōmôt*] of the earth
> > you will bring me up again. (71:20)

In Ps. 42 the poet has not only been overwhelmed by waves, but is also sinking in the bottomless depths, from which he cries out for help:

> Deep calls to deep [*tᵉhôm 'el tᵉhôm qôrē'*]
> > at the thunder of your cataracts;
> all your waves and your billows
> > have gone over me. (42:7)

When those who go down to the sea in ships encounter storms and gigantic waves, they feel they are sinking into *tᵉhōmôt* and their courage melts away, (107:26).

Other, less striking, words which have much the same meaning (*ma'ᵃmaqqîm* and *mᵉṣûlāh* or *mᵉṣôlāh*) are also used to express personal distress. The poet of Ps. 69 complains twice of being in 'deep waters' (or 'the depths') vv. 2, 14, and once of the fear of being swallowed up by the 'deep' v. 15:

> I have come into deep waters, [or 'the depths' *ma'ᵃmaqqîm*]
> > and the flood sweeps over me. (v. 2)

> Let me be delivered from my enemies
> > and from the deep waters [*ma'ᵃmaqqîm*]. (v. 14)
> Do not let the flood sweep over me,
> > or the deep [*mᵉṣûlāh*] swallow me up,
> > or the Pit close its mouth over me. (v. 15)

And one of these words is found also in the famous *De Profundis*, Ps. 130:

> Out of the depths [*ma'ᵃmaqqîm*] I cry to you, O LORD.
> > Lord, hear my voice! (v. 1)

The depths is a place of bottomless human suffering, a place where one is overwhelmed and in danger of sinking, where life can disintegrate into chaos, and where all one can do is cry out to God for help.

The Pit and Sheol

The image of the deep is also related to the image of the Pit,[24] the mysterious abyss which lies below human life. More than once the depths and the Pit are found together in poetic parallelism:

> You have put me in the depths of the Pit, [*bôr*]
>> in the regions of the depths [*m^{e}sōlôt*, 'regions dark and deep'
>> NRSV] (88:6; see 69:15 above)

We saw earlier that the pit can refer to a cistern in which a person can sink and be overwhelmed. But it is also something more intangible; the subterranean abyss, the Pit of nothingness which is underneath the earth, sometimes referred to as 'the depths of the earth' (63:9; 71:20). The deep, the place of floods and overwhelming waves, is also this Pit of emptiness.

And the Pit in turn is closely connected with the idea of death, as can be seen from its frequent use as a synonym for Sheol, the abode of the dead:

> O LORD, you brought up my soul from Sheol,
>> restored me to life from among those gone down to the Pit.
>> (30:3)

> My soul is full of troubles,
>> and my life draws near to Sheol.
> I am counted among those who go down to the Pit;
>> I am like those who have no help. (88:3–4)

> For you do not give me up to Sheol,
>> or let your faithful one see the Pit. (16:10)

Sheol, which is mentioned frequently in the Psalms, was a subterranean region to which the dead go down. It was a dark, gloomy region where the dead existed as mere shades. Those who 'went down to Sheol' had a 'soulless shadowy existence far removed from God' in 'a land which is not a land'.[25] Although it may be seen as a mythological concept, it was regarded as a definite place. The rabbis and later Jewish interpreters called it 'the Lower World' or 'Gehenna', the place of punishment.[26] It could be viewed figuratively as a city, with 'gates' (9:13; Isa. 38:10).

Since it is the place of death or of the dead, it can appear directly as a synonym for death:

> For in death there is no remembrance of you;
>> in Sheol who can give you praise? (6:5)

> Let death come upon them;
>> let them go down alive to Sheol. (55:15; see also 49:14; 89:48)

'The Pit', 'Sheol' and 'death' could thus be used interchangeably, and the idea of the 'deep' overlaps with all of them.

Sometimes Sheol or death was personified. Perhaps under the influence of the old Canaanite myth of Mot, the god of death, Sheol or death could be seen as a greedy monster which could take hold of people and trap them in its snare:

> The cords of Sheol entangled me;
>> the snares of death confronted me. (18:5; see also 116:3)

And like a greedy monster, death could swallow its victims. Being over-whelmed by the waters of the great deep could be compared with being swallowed by the Pit, as we saw in a verse already quoted:

> Do not let the flood sweep over me,
>> or the deep swallow me up,
>> or the Pit close its mouth over me. (69:15)

The same idea seems to be present in Ps. 18:4 which speaks of 'torrents of perdition', where the word 'perdition', *beliyya'al*, (perhaps connected with the verb *b-l-'*, 'to swallow') is 'likely to be another title of Death, the Swallower, closely allied with the waters of chaos'.[27] Elsewhere in the Old Testament Sheol is said to swallow people alive (Prov. 1:12). The monster death had a voracious appetite. As in the Canaanite myth, where the god Mot declares that it was natural for him to 'eat with both my hands',[28] so in the Old Testament Sheol and death can 'never have enough' and 'are never satisfied' (Hab. 2:5; Prov. 27:20; see also Prov. 30:15f). Or in another personified image, death is like a shepherd gathering people into Sheol, its fold:

> Like sheep they are appointed for Sheol;
>> Death shall be their shepherd. (49:14)

This envisaging of death as a person adds a special measure of terror to the image of the Pit.

But Sheol and the Pit are more usually thought of as a place into which people had to descend. In near eastern mythology death was a matter of going *down* to a region below,[29] and in the Psalms the phrase 'to go down to the Pit' is a common way of referring to dying (28:1; 30:3, 9; 88:4; 143:7). Sheol was a region over which death reigned, a territory which was separate from the territory of life over which God reigned, a place into which everyone ultimately descended. But although these were separate territories or spheres, significantly, the sphere of death was understood to be constantly encroaching on the sphere of life. Death had an influence not only in the land of Sheol but also in the land of the living. Sheol was a 'territory hostile to life',[30] which posed a constant threat to the living. Anything that diminished, impaired or threatened the fullness of life was seen as an encroachment of death. Any form of suffering, any misery, weakness or disease, was a form of death. Thus to be in the Pit, or to go down to Sheol was not necessarily to die in the complete sense. It meant to be 'face to face with the power of death, and physical death is only an extreme case, different in degree but not in kind from all the other threats to human life'.[31] Death and Sheol were present in the midst of life. So one could be in the Pit or in Sheol and be brought up again without having died in the physical sense. Thus the poet of Ps. 88 could say:

> I am counted among those who go down to the Pit . . .
>   You have put me in the depths of the Pit. (88:4, 6)

And the poet of Ps. 30 could rejoice at being brought up again from the Sheol:

> O LORD, you brought up my soul from Sheol,
>   restored me to life from among those gone down to the Pit. (30:3)

The key to understanding this is to recognise that for the psalmists God was the God of life and of the living, and not of the dead. Those who had died and gone down to Sheol were separated from God. They were in the territory ruled by death, not in the territory of the living ruled by God. 'Sheol . . . and the living God necessarily exclude one another. The dwelling of death is the dwelling of death because Yhwh is not there.'[32] All attempts by death, therefore, to snatch at those in life and drag them towards Sheol, whether through sickness or some other form of distress, were attempts to separate people from God. Death and the encroachment of death through illness or disaster were not only forms of suffering or misery, they were a cutting off from the land of the living, and a separation from the God of life. Sheol or the Pit was, in other words, a place of God-forsakenness,33 a place where one was abandoned by God.

It was this that gave its terror to the Pit. The image of the great abyss carried with it the fear of being forsaken and separated from God, the source of all life and goodness. And it is this which gives colour to all the imagery in this cluster. The images we have considered – the muddy cistern, the waves and floods, the great waters, the unfathomable deep – all speak no doubt of human suffering of various kinds. The imagery can be used to give expression to all sorts of troubles which overwhelm human beings and bring chaos into their lives. But running through them all is the greatest terror, the fear of separation from God. It was this that made all forms of human suffering so terribly fearful, because they all were to a greater or lesser degree a partaking in death, an experience of God-forsakenness. They are all encroachments of the kingdom of death.

Images of Evil

With this we return to the theme of evil. Do the images we have discussed in this chapter point to any other ways of understanding evil and the way it operates? If the imagery of the previous chapter pointed to evil as something both beyond us and within us which attacks and spoils human life, the imagery of this chapter suggests that evil can perhaps be viewed in two further ways. It can be seen, on the one hand, as something which, like the waters of the primordial deep, brings chaos and disorder to human life, and which threatens to destroy the order of God's creation. On the other hand, evil can be understood as the encroachment of the sphere of death into human life in the form of suffering and misery, and which in this way threatens to separate human beings from God, the source of life. It is perhaps its power to threaten God's order on the one hand, and to bring human beings into a place of forsakenness by God on the other, that makes evil what it is. We will have to consider in a later chapter the implication of these points for our understanding of evil, and of the relationship between evil and suffering. For the moment, we will pursue in the next chapter some other images which form a third cluster.

Chapter 7

Images of Distress: (3) Separation from God

The images of the third cluster have to do with separation from God. They may perhaps be less graphic than some we have looked at, but they point nevertheless to something which is central to an understanding of evil. We will look at four images in this cluster.

Being Far Off

Being away from God may not seem like an image at all. It has perhaps become a stock or even a dead metaphor, one which has been used so often that it is no longer consciously felt to be a metaphor.[1] Nevertheless, if we recall that the phrase is basically a metaphorical one, describing a spiritual condition in terms of physical distance, this will enable us to make some useful connections with other poetic images.

Many psalms speak in one way or another of being far away from God, usually in the form of a plea to God not to be far off:

> O LORD, do not be far from me! (35:22)

> O my God, do not be far from me. (38:21)

> Do not be far from me,
>   for trouble is near
>   and there is no one to help. (22:11)

> But you, O LORD, do not be far away!
>   O my help, come quickly to my aid! (22:19)

> O God, do not be far from me;
>   O my God, make haste to help me! (71:12)

People undergoing deep distress were inclined to feel that they were remote from God, and so they called out to him to be near. Sometimes their sense of remoteness was expressed by referring to geographically distant places, as if the psalmist was physically far away from God. Thus Ps. 61 speaks rather vaguely of being at 'the end of the earth':

> From the end of the earth I call to you,
>   when my heart is faint. (61:2)

We need not assume from this (as some commentators do) that at the time of writing the psalmist was in some physically distant location. Rather, the end of the earth can be seen as a place of terrible distress, 'the remote outermost place' of human affliction.[2] This point is underlined by the fact that the verb 'to be faint' in this verse ('-*ṭ*-*p*) is one which is quite commonly used of extreme distress (77:3; 102: title; 107:5; 142:3; 143:4; see also Jonah 2:7). Or perhaps the end of the earth may be 'an expression . . . for the entrance of the Underworld'.[3] Being in the midst of troubles or at the gates of death, the psalmist felt as far removed from God as it was possible to be. Metaphorically he was at the end of the earth.

The same may be said of psalms which refer by name to particular places; this too may well be a metaphorical way of describing a sense of distress and of being distant from God. The much-discussed words of Ps. 42:6,

> My soul is cast down within me;
>   therefore I remember you
> from the land of Jordan and of Hermon,
>   from Mount Mizar,

are sometimes taken to indicate that the psalmist found himself beside the source of the Jordan at Mount Hermon in the far north of Palestine, a place of rushing water and cataracts.[4] But it may be better to regard them as a graphic metaphor for a situation of being far removed from God. Being overwhelmed by troubles as by waves and billows (v. 7), the psalmist feels himself to be in a far distant place, separated from God. The same may be true of Ps. 120:5:

> Woe is me, that I am an alien in Meshech,
>   that I must live among the tents of Kedar.

The fact that Meshech and Kedar are geographically a long way distant from each other makes it likely that the psalmist was using them as metaphors for a sense of spiritual remoteness, and feelings of deep inner distress.

Behind this feeling of being far removed from God there lay the belief in two opposing realms, referred to in the previous chapter. There was, on the one hand the territory or domain of God, 'the good sphere of Yhwh' where God ruled and was present. And on the other hand there was the territory or domain of evil, 'an evil sphere, a realm of Death and chaos'[5] which stood against the domain of God and constantly threatened it. Since God was the source of life, to be near God or in his domain was to be in the realm of life and of goodness. To be in the domain of evil was to be separated from God and under the rule of death. In their distress the psalmists felt themselves to be in danger of being drawn into this realm far away from God; and so they cried out to him to 'be not far'. Correspondingly, when they were relieved of their distress they felt themselves once more to be in the 'land of the living':

> You have delivered my soul from death,
>> my eyes from tears,
>> my feet from stumbling.
> I will walk before the LORD
>> in the land of the living. (116:8–9)

The temple in Jerusalem had an important part in this. In it God was understood to be present in a special way. Devout Israelites would come to the temple in order to 'appear before God', or to 'behold the face of God'. It was 'the manifest expression for his sacramental presence among humankind'.[6] In this way the temple, together with the 'holy hill' on which it stood, was a vital and visible symbol of the good sphere or territory of Yhwh. The 'courts of the LORD' were the physical manifestation of the realm of God and of life, which was opposed to the realm of evil and death. So when the psalmists were in distress and felt far removed from God they longed for the temple, the visible sign of his realm:

> When shall I come and behold the face of God? (42:2)

> O send out your light and your truth;
>> let them lead me;
> let them bring me to your holy hill
>> and to your dwelling. (43:3)

When they were beset by foes, the powers of evil, it was from his holy hill that they sought help:

> O LORD, how many are my foes!

Many are rising against me.
I cry aloud to the LORD,
    and he answers me from his holy hill. (3:1, 4)

The image of physical distance was, therefore, a powerful one. To be far from God was not simply a source of discomfort, it was a matter of life and death. 'Those who are far from you will perish' (73:27). By its implied reference to the territory of evil and death, far removed from the sphere of God and life, it expressed the extreme distress which arose from being cut off from God. It may therefore be seen as another way of speaking figuratively and graphically of evil.

The image of being far off is also connected with another and rather different thought, that of being forsaken by God.

Do not forsake me, O LORD;
    O my God, do not be far from me. (38:21)

My God, my God, why have you forsaken me?
    Why are you so far from helping me [literally, 'from my help']?
(22:1)

In their distress the psalmists could sometimes attribute their remoteness from God not to the encroachments of evil but to God himself. When the sense of separation was particularly acute, they felt that God had abandoned them. When distress had come upon them he seemed to be far away, and had not come to their rescue. That is to say, God was felt to be responsible, in some measure at least, for the situation in which they found themselves.

Slipping and Stumbling

Another image which speaks of separation from God is that of one's foot slipping, or of stumbling and falling:

My steps have held fast to your paths;
    my feet have not slipped. (17:5)

The image here comes from the mountains, and envisages steep hill paths in rough and stony country, such as the hill country of Judah. In such conditions to slip or stumble was dangerous, as a fall down the steep hillside could be fatal. Stumbling or slipping was not some minor mishap, but a disaster which could lead to death. The image is thus a powerful one, speaking of a real danger to life. Sometimes psalmists simply tell of the danger of slipping, without expanding the image:

> But as for me, my feet had almost stumbled;
>> my steps had nearly slipped. (73:2)

More often they recall with thankfulness that it is God who keeps them from stumbling and falling:

> When I thought, 'My foot is slipping',
>> your steadfast love, O LORD, held me up. (94:18)

> You gave me a wide place for my steps under me,
>> and my feet did not slip. (18:36)

> He will not let your foot be moved (or 'slip'). (121:3)

In using this image the psalmists did not, of course, have in mind the physical danger of slipping and falling, but a profound spiritual danger. To stumble is a threat to one's very existence, and is associated with tears and with death:

> For you have delivered my soul from death,
>> and my feet from falling,
> so that I may walk before God
>> in the light of life. (56:13, see also 116:8f quoted above)

> Bless our God, O peoples . . .
>> who has kept us among the living,
>> and has not let our feet slip. (66:8–9)

To fall is to be removed from the land of the living, and to be saved from falling is to keep one's place among the living. To understand the importance of this imagery we have to recognise that its background is once again the two realms, the realm of God and life, and the realm of evil and death. Stumbling is dangerous because to fall is to be transferred from the realm of God which is the sphere of life, and cast into the realm of evil which is the sphere of death. Conversely, if one is saved from stumbling one is kept in life, or in the land of the living.

Additional colour is given to the image by the use in 116:8 and 56:13 of the Hebrew word *dᵉḥî*, translated 'stumbling'. This is a very unusual word, which is associated with the verb *d-ḥ-h*, to push or thrust, (see especially 118:13; 140:4). It suggests that perhaps the stumbling which the psalmist feared was a matter of being thrust from the path by enemies who were watching his steps (56:6) and trying to bring about his downfall. Here the image of slipping is linked with that of the enemies. Stumbling is not just an accident: it is caused by 'impious attacks' which 'have a demonic character'.[7] Elsewhere the enemies, the insidious malevolent forces of evil, are pictured as surrounding the psalmist, rubbing their hands with boasting and glee if he slips and falls:

> But at my stumbling they gathered in glee,
> > they gathered together against me. (35:15)

> For I pray, 'Only do not let them rejoice over me,
> > those who boast against me when my foot slips.'
> For I am ready to fall. (38:16–17)

When one's foot slips the enemies have occasion to rejoice because one has been inveigled into evil, and drawn into the realm of death.

This way of understanding slipping or stumbling is reinforced if we look at the main Hebrew word which these words translate. The verb *m-w-ṭ* means principally 'to totter', 'to move', 'to shake', or (in its passive or niphal form) 'to be moved'. It is often used of people. It is said of the 'righteous' (112:6) and of those who 'walk blamelessly and do what is right' (15:2) that they 'shall never be moved' (or 'never stumble', 15:5). Those who remain in the presence of God and trust wholly in him can have confidence that they will not be moved:

> I keep the LORD always before me;
> > because he is at my right hand, I shall not be moved. (16:8)

> He alone is my rock and my salvation,
> > my fortress; I shall never be shaken [or moved]. (62:2, 6)

On the other hand, those who believe that their prosperity can save them from being moved may be in for a shock:

> As for me, I said in my prosperity,
> > 'I shall never be moved.' . . .
> You hid your face;
> > I was dismayed. (30:6–7)

Being moved is clearly a serious danger, and one from which only God can save. Just how serious it is can be seen from the fact that it threatens not only individual people, but the world itself. There is a danger that 'the earth should change', and 'the mountains shake ['be moved'] in the heart of the sea' (46:2). It is only because the LORD provides his protection that Mount Zion, his dwelling place, cannot be moved:

> Those who trust in the LORD are like Mount Zion,
>   which cannot be moved, but abides for ever. (125:1)

It is because the LORD is king that the world itself cannot be moved:

> Say among the nations, 'The LORD is king!
>   The world is firmly established; it shall never be moved'. (96:10)

There is something cosmic about the threat of being moved or stumbling. For the world as a whole, as for the individual person, to stumble or to totter is to fall into a realm of chaos and evil. There is a danger that the earth could slip into the chaos which, as we saw in the last chapter, continues to threaten the cosmic order. When the demonic powers, represented by the 'gods', are out of control, 'all the foundations of the earth are shaken [or moved]' (Ps. 82:5). 'The demonic power plays of the gods call the existence of the world into question. Chaos threatens to break in.'[8] If the earth is moved, or if a person's feet slip or stumble, this is because evil is attempting to seize the world and its inhabitants for its realm, and to draw them down into chaos. But so long as people's 'feet stand secure on the holy rock of God',[9] so long as they remain within God's territory without slipping, they are safe from the clutches of evil. Not to be moved is, in Davidson's words, 'the privilege of being in God's presence'.[10]

The image of slipping, stumbling or being moved is thus a further way of representing the threat of evil. Once again the evil lies in being separated from God, in falling out of God's realm and the sphere of life, into the realm of chaos and death.

Imprisonment and Bondage

The image of being in prison or bonds is also connected with separation from God, although perhaps more loosely. The word 'prisoner' can, of course, be taken to refer to people who were literally in captivity, as is apparently the case in, for example, 68:6; 79:11 and 107:10. But even here there may be a metaphorical meaning alongside a literal one, and in other psalms a figurative sense is even more clearly required. Reference to imprisonment or bondage often occurs alongside other images of distress, in a way which shows that it too can be a metaphorical way of describing the psalmist's troubles. Ps. 69, for instance, speaks of distress in terms of sinking in deep waters, and the threat of enemies, and then it adds

> For the LORD hears the needy,
>   and does not despise his own that are in bonds. (v. 33)

In the same way, Ps. 116 praises God for deliverance from death, tears and stumbling (v. 8, quoted above), and goes on to conclude that 'you have loosed my bonds' (v. 16). The final verse of Ps. 142,

> Bring me out of prison,
>> so that I may give thanks to your name.
> The righteous will surround me,
>> for you will deal bountifully with me (v. 7)

has led many commentators to believe that the composer of the psalm was literally a prisoner. But the reference to prison follows verses which speak of persecutors and hidden traps (vv. 3, 6) which are common images of distress (see Chapter 4). The image of being in prison conveys an acute feeling of being shut in, confined or restricted, of being in a situation from which there is no escape, and so, like the other images we have been examining, it is a way of describing the experience of severe trouble and distress.

One can, of course, be restricted or confined in various ways, and the sense of being shut in is found in a number of psalms even where there is no reference to prison or bonds. It is given particularly powerful expression in two of the most poignant psalms of complaint, Pss 22 and 88. Ps. 22 speaks vividly of being 'surrounded' and therefore shut in on all sides, by wild beasts or by enemies:

> Many bulls encircle me,
>> strong bulls of Bashan surround me;
> they open wide their mouths at me,
>> like a ravening and roaring lion. (vv. 12–13)

> For dogs are all around me;
>> a company of evildoers encircles me. (v. 16)

The bulls, lions, dogs and evildoers are, as we have seen, themselves graphic images of danger, distress and evil, but the threat which they pose is especially severe because they surround or encircle the sufferer. They are terrifying because they shut the person in so that there is no escape. Ps. 88 is perhaps of all the psalms the one which expresses the greatest sense of despair. Various images which we have examined, including the Pit and Sheol, waves and floods, are used here, but along with them there is the acute sense of being shut in:

> You have caused my companions to shun me;
>> you have made me a thing of horror to them.
> I am shut in so that I cannot escape. (v. 8)

Your wrath has swept over me;
   your dread assaults destroy me.
They surround me like a flood all day long;
   from all sides they close in on me. (vv. 16–17)

The same idea is found in other psalms: Ps. 17 tells of being tracked down and surrounded by deadly enemies, (v. 11); Ps. 40 of being encompassed or surrounded by 'evils without number' (v. 12); Ps. 109 of being beset or surrounded by 'wicked and deceitful mouths' (vv. 2–3). Being surrounded and shut in with no means of escape is thus a common way of describing distress, and the image of prison or bondage gives especially vivid expression to this.

To be surrounded and shut in means not just to be restricted but to be cut off or separated. The poet of Ps. 88 was cut off from his companions, and those in prison would be separated from home and family and the ordinary things of life. So here again we have distress expressed in terms of separation. To be in prison, to be shut in, or surrounded by forces from which one cannot escape is a way of expressing the distress which comes from being cut off from God. And since this image is closely associated with others, such as enemies, wild beasts, floods and the Pit, which represent the attacks and the overwhelming power of the forces of evil, it can be read as a metaphor of the separation from God which is brought about by evil.

To understand prison and bonds in this way adds a further dimension of meaning to other psalms which refer to prisoners. Just as in Ps. 107 the 'great waters' which endanger the lives of those who go 'down to the sea in ships' may represent not only the physical ocean with its dangers but also the primeval chaos which threatens to engulf the world and its peoples (see p. 65); so in the same psalm those who

   . . . sat in darkness and in gloom,
      prisoners in misery and in irons, (v. 10)

may be seen not as those taken captive by a hostile army or put in prison for their misdeeds, but as people who had been ensnared by the forces of evil. They were those who, by the very fact that they

   . . . had rebelled against the words of God,
      and spurned the counsel of the Most High, (v. 11)

had fallen into the grip of evil and had been cut off from God, until he 'broke their bonds asunder' (v. 14). Similarly, when Ps. 68 declares that

God 'leads out the prisoners to prosperity' (v. 6), and Ps. 146 that 'the LORD sets the prisoners free' (v. 7), and when Ps. 79 calls on God to 'Let the groans of the prisoners come before you' (v. 11), they may be referring literally to people taken captive; but lurking behind the literal reference there may also be the thought of people who are shut in and cut off from God. To be a prisoner is not simply to be denied one's physical freedom, but to be separated from God.

God Hides His Face

This image is both a moving and a mysterious one. The 'face' (*pānîm*) is the regular Hebrew way of referring to presence. To say that God hides his face is therefore a graphic way of saying that he withdraws his presence, and so it is a powerful way of expressing a sense of separation from God. For the psalmists, of course, God was in one sense always present. Ps. 139 emphasises the fact that no one could escape from the all-present and all-seeing God:

> Where can I go from your spirit?
> Or where can I flee from your presence [or 'face']? (139:7)

Moreover, as we have seen, the temple in Jerusalem was felt to be a representation and a guarantee of the presence of God. Nevertheless from time to time the psalmists also experienced something which seemed like the absence of God, the hiding of his face. In psalms of deep distress we repeatedly find them calling out, 'Do not hide your face from me' or 'from your servant' (27:9; 69:17; 102:2; 143:7). In times of trouble God no longer seemed to be present. Or perhaps it was the very hiding of God's face which actually caused their trouble.

However it came about, the hiding of God's face was experienced as painful and terrifying. God was the source of life, goodness and security, and when he withdrew his presence or hid his face all sorts of terrible and evil things could happen. Without God's presence all creatures were in danger of death:

> When you hide your face, they are dismayed;
> when you take away their breath, they die,
> and return to their dust. (104:29)

And for the individual the hiding of God's face could bring about the experience of being dragged down towards the Pit, perhaps through illness:

> You hid your face;
>> I was dismayed.
> To you, O LORD, I cried,
>> and to the LORD I made supplication:
> 'What profit is there in my death,
>> if I go down to the Pit?' (30:7–9)

There is in the Psalms a sense of bewilderment about the hiding of God's face: the psalmists cannot understand why it happens. The same is not true of the prophets: for them the hiding of God's face takes place because of the wickedness of the people; their sin causes God to withdraw his presence:

> I have hidden my face from this city because of all their
> wickedness. (Jer. 33:5)

> Then they will cry to the LORD,
>> but he will not answer them;
> he will hide his face from them at that time,
>> because they have acted wickedly. (Mic. 3:4, see also Isa. 54:8;
>> 59:2; 64:7; Ezek. 39:23)

In the Psalms, however, it is not because of the people's sin that God hides his face.[11] No reason is given for God's withdrawal, so that the psalmists find themselves puzzled and bewildered by his absence. They are not aware of sin or wickedness on their part, and so cannot understand why God has hidden his face. If, as in Ps. 30, the hiding of his face was 'a picturesque expression of displeasure and of the withdrawal of the divine favour' leading to sickness and suffering,[12] there was no apparent reason for this displeasure. In these circumstances, all the psalmist could do was to call out 'Why?':

> O LORD, why do you cast me off?
>> Why do you hide your face from me? (88:14)

> Our heart has not turned back,
>> nor have our steps departed from your way . . .
> Why do you hide your face? (44:18, 24)

But there is an even greater mystery about the hiding of God's face. God's withdrawal sometimes allows the enemy to triumph, and so in a sense gives opportunity to evil:

> How long will you hide your face from me? . . .
> How long shall my enemy be exalted over me? (13:1, 2)

The hiding of God's face makes it possible for the wicked to do their evil deeds:

> They think in their heart, 'God has forgotten,
> he has hidden his face, he will never see it.' (10:11)

If the action of God in withdrawing his face is not said to be the cause of evil, it at least provides an opportunity for it. The separation from God may be brought about by evil but somehow God seems at least to go along with it. As we saw in Chapter 4, there is a deep mystery here which the psalmists cannot explain. All they can do is protest to God about it.

All the images we have considered in this chapter have expressed in different ways what it is like to be separated or cut off from God: it is like being in a distant place far removed from the place of God's presence; or being shut away in prison; or stumbling on the rocky hill path and falling out of the realm of God; or living with God's face turned away. Although they leave many questions unanswered, they tell us something about the psalmists' understanding of evil. Taken together with the images in the other clusters, they can be used to build up a general picture of what evil was like and how it operated for the psalmists, and it is to this we turn in the next chapter.

Chapter 8

Evil in the Psalms: A Summary

Up to now we have been looking at images. By their very nature poetic images do not make explicit what they are referring to, and so are open to various interpretations. The images of distress in the Psalms do not refer directly to evil, but we have seen that they can be interpreted as saying something about evil. It is now time to gather up and summarise what has emerged from our discussion of these various images, and to say some general things about how the psalmists understood evil.

An Independent Reality

A first point to which the imagery directs us is that evil is a power which is both suprahuman and, in some measure at least, independent of God. As we saw in Chapter 5, the image of the 'great waters' and of the sea monster or dragon, drawn from ancient mythology, gives us a picture of such a power. It refers to the primordial chaos which was there before the creation, and which God overcame at the creation of the cosmos. The use of the language of myth to refer to this power shows it to be mysterious and incomprehensible, something vicious like a dragon, unfathomable like the great deep, and threatening like overwhelming waves. It is an evil power opposed to God.

By portraying it in this way the psalmists and others make it clear that evil for them was not just something in the human mind or heart: there was what Paul Ricoeur, in a study of evil with special reference to the Old Testament, has called a 'radical externality of evil, a cosmic structure of evil'.[1] It was non-human and not caused by God. The powers of evil were, in von Rad's words, 'uncreated powers'.[2] While traditional Christian and Jewish theology has maintained that the world was created out of nothing, *ex nihilo*, and that everything that is owes its origin entirely to God, there is much in the Old Testament which suggests that the power of chaos was apparently there quite independently of God. According to Levenson, the 'formless void' (*tōhû wābōhû*, Gen. 1:2) from which the world was made, was not 'nothing' in the sense of non-being. To the ancients,

> 'nothing' was something – something negative. It was not the privation of being ... but a real, active force, except that its charge was entirely negative ... they identified 'nothing' with things like disorder, injustice, subjugation, disease and death.[3]

Similarly, Brueggemann argues that

> we are bound to conclude that Israel understood Yhwh's activity of creation to be one of forming, shaping, governing, ordering and sustaining a created world out of the 'stuff of chaos,' which was already there.[4]

'It would perhaps be more appropriate,' says Kraus, 'to speak of a "creatio contra nihilum," if *nihil* includes the abyss of chaos, the primeval chaotic power.'[5] That is to say, psalmists and other Old Testament writers seem to accept a primordial or cosmic dualism,[6] a belief that there is 'a deliberate anti-God power'[7] at work. Writing of the individual complaint psalms Lindström maintains that

> the understanding of life which these psalms presuppose has a dualistic nature, that is, it presupposes that the threat toward human existence is made up of a supraindividual evil.[8]

That is not to say that the psalmists believed in a personal devil. Such a belief came later, at a time after most of the psalms were written. The devil is first mentioned in Jewish literature in the fourth century BCE, in the course of attempts to explain the origin of evil.[9] The psalmists could refer to evil in mythological language, but they had no concept of it as a person in the form of a devil. Their language suggests instead that although it was mysterious and sinister, it was not a personal force, but something subhuman and impersonal.

But, of course, the psalmists also believed that at the creation God had overcome this hostile power. The imagery of the sea and the dragon was used to emphasise God's triumph over primordial chaos (74:13–15; 89:9–10; 93:3–4). When the psalms used in the Jerusalem cult celebrated God's 'victory', it was no doubt to this triumph that they were referring.[10] The psalmists were convinced of the superiority of God's power over that of chaos or evil, but this victory was thought of and described in different ways. As well as telling of the battle with the dragons, the psalms also speak of the sea being confined within its appropriate limits or bounds (104:9); or put in storehouses (33:7); or its waves stilled and its roaring silenced (65:7). Sometimes the victory was related to the story of the Exodus from Egypt (66:6; 77:16–20; 78:13; 114:1; 136:13), and spoken of in terms of the rebuking, dividing, drying up or restraining of the sea. All of these descriptions can be seen as 'a translation of the mythical action of the killing or annihilating the tyrant.'[11]

By his victory, therefore, God has broken the power of primordial chaos. There is no doubt that evil is subject to God. Nevertheless, our discussion of this imagery in Chapter 6 also made it apparent that God has not totally removed evil. It has been defeated in the cosmic struggle, and confined within its limits, but it has not been completely eliminated. It is still possible for the world to 'slip out of God's control and into the hands of obscure but potent forces of malignancy'.[12] For the psalmists and other biblical writers evil, although subordinate to God, is still a present reality. It is a mysterious reality, which can neither be described in words of rational prose, nor explained in terms of philosophical thought, but which can only be pointed to by using the language of metaphor and myth. The same way of thinking and speaking about evil can be found in the New Testament. When Paul (or one of his followers) talks of 'principalities' and 'powers' (Eph. 6:12, RSV) or 'the elemental spirits of the universe' (Col. 2:8; Gal. 4:3), he 'is using mythical language of great antiquity and con- tinuing vitality'.[13] The language of myth can point, as we have seen, to a reality which is transcendent and beyond our full comprehension. For their part the psalmists used the image of the dragon and the many waters to convey an idea of evil as a malignant power, independent of God, defeated by him at creation, but continuing to pose a threat to the order and well-being of the world.

A Hostile Reality

This independent power of evil was clearly seen as hostile in its intentions. The imagery of the great waters of chaos and of the dragon conveyed something of this hostility. Chaos was, in von Rad's words, '*the* great menace to creation',[14] and hostility was also represented through the image of the enemies which symbolised the forces of evil. The psalmists can often combine or mix their metaphors, so that the images of the waters and the enemies can occur together, forming different ways of represent- ing hostility (18:16–17; 69:14; 124:2–5).

This hostility has three objects. firstly, it is directed against God himself.

The fact that there was a battle between God and the chaos dragon presupposes a basic hostility between the two. Similarly the enemies spoken of in the psalms are primarily the enemies of God (37:20; 66:3; 68:1; 83:2; 89:10; 92:9, see p. 41 above). There is an 'enemy and avenger' that is opposed to the power of God (8:2). The powers of evil still have God as their principal opponent, and it is from this prior and primary hostility to God that the hostility of the enemies towards humans arises.

Secondly, the hostility of evil is directed against human society and its order. The frequent portrayal of the enemies as hostile foreign nations should be understood in this way. The hostile powers which threatened and attacked the people of God were symbols of the forces of evil which threatened to disrupt good order in the political and social realm. Since in the ancient world a nation was identified with its gods, the nations surrounding Israel were equated with the false gods which were in opposition to Yhwh, the God of Israel. In Ps. 82 these gods are apparently part of the hostile force of evil. 'It is these other gods,' says Davidson, 'who must accept responsibility for the evil on earth'.[15] When the psalmists spoke of the nations as enemies, therefore, they were not simply indulging in xenophobia, but were viewing these nations as representatives of the evil powers.

By speaking of evil in terms of a battle between Israel and its neighbours, the psalmists make it clear that evil is something hostile not only to God, but also to God's people and human society. The battle against evil was not only God's original battle against primordial chaos, but also a struggle taking place within the subsequent life of the world. It was because of this that the chaos myth of the battle with the dragon was, in Mowinckel's phrase, 'mutated' into a myth about the fight against the nations.[16] As we have seen, the ancient chaos myth was historicised and applied to events in the history of God's people, principally the Exodus from Egypt and the exile to Babylon. The identification of Egypt and Babylon with Rahab the mythical sea dragon was a graphic way of asserting that, throughout Israel's history, evil continued to be a threat to its life and to the just ordering of human society. The hostility to God of the sea dragon and the power of chaos was perpetuated in the continued hostility of the nations against God's people.

Thirdly, the enemies were also a threat to the individual. We encounter them most of all in the individual psalms of complaint, where they are often spoken of in very personal terms. To take but one example, Ps. 13 connects the 'enemy' with a very inwardly felt distress:

> How long must I bear pain in my soul,
>   and have sorrow in my heart all day long?
> How long shall my enemy be exalted over me? (13:2)

Those who regard the 'I' of these psalms as the king speaking in the name of his people, or as some kind of 'corporate personality', will of course reject the purely personal reference. But if in the Psalms the enemies are the forces of evil which are in opposition first of all to God, and then to the good order of society, there is no reason to believe that they are not in a very real and personal sense enemies of the individual as well. Whether through sickness or disaster, through treachery or the actions of 'evil-doers', the insidious power of evil could threaten the well-being and even the life of individual people by attacking them in their inmost being, their soul or heart.

The psalmists, therefore, portray evil as a malicious power whose hostility is asserted in various ways. By their image of the enemies they describe figuratively the continued activity in the life of the world of the power of chaos and evil. In so doing they give us a graphic picture of the fact that this power operates both in society and in individuals.

Separation and Death

If, then, evil is a hostile power, how does it harm human beings and society? It is clear from the Psalms that the power of evil to threaten and disrupt human life lies in its ability to separate people from God. It is the presence of God that gives life and blessing. In his presence there is fullness of joy (16:11). Ultimately there is nothing to be desired other than this (73:25). To be with God or near God is the ultimate good, and the goal of life. Conversely, the absence of God is the source of all affliction and sorrow. To be separated from God is the greatest of all disasters. It is this that causes the psalmists to plead with God not to be far from them, and that lends power to the images of slipping, of being shut off and imprisoned, and of the hiding of God's face. The danger posed by the hostile power of evil, by primeval chaos on the one hand and by enemies in various forms on the other, is that it could wrench human beings away from the presence of God.

This experience of separation, or of 'God-forsakenness'[17] is the ultimate depth of human desolation. It is to have a fearful sense of nothingness, of sinking in the depths to which there is no bottom; it is to encounter what Brueggemann calls 'the Nihil'.[18] It is this experience which causes the psalmists to cry out

> My God, my God, why have you forsaken me? (22:1)

or

> How long, O LORD? Will you forget me for ever?
> How long will you hide your face from me? (13:1)

'This most desperate and bitter state of mind', as Luther calls it,[19] is the result of a sense that one is abandoned by God and separated from him.

We have seen that the psalmists figuratively envisage this separation spatially. In their view there was a realm of evil and death which existed and was set against the realm of God and life. God's realm was symbolised by Mount Zion, the holy hill of God, where people of godliness and purity were to be found (15:1–2; 24:3–4). The temple, the 'house' of God on Mount Zion, was the special place of his presence and a source of joy and gladness (43:4; 122:1). It was the desire of all godly people to 'dwell in God's house forever' (23:6; 27:4). But the forces of evil attempted to draw people away into the realm of evil, where they were held prisoner, far from God. And it was the aim of these forces to cause the feet of those who walked the hill paths of God's country to slip or be moved so that they fell into the territory of evil and absence of God.

This realm of evil was also Sheol, the place of death and the abode of the dead. Death was the arch-enemy of humankind, causing the final severance from God and life, which was the ultimate evil. In Sheol God was not present; there was no remembrance of God. It was thus the ultimate place of separation or God-forsakenness. But Sheol, the territory of death, also extended its grasp towards the living. Illness, weakness or calamity were experienced as the encroachment of Sheol, the grip of death on those who were still in the land of the living. Evil thus penetrated into the midst of human life, attempting always to cut people off from God. It was both the power which presided over the realm of death, and the power which drew people down towards it. It threatened to cause the whole world to be moved or shaken, to bring ruin and disorder, and separate the world from its Creator.

Stealth and Seduction

Evil, then, was a hostile enemy, threatening to cut the world and its people off from God. It did not, however, work overtly in an obvious way, but stealthily and secretly. According to the psalmists, it drew people down to the world of death not by force, but with cunning and deception. This can be seen from the images of the snares and traps and hidden pitfalls, and from the fact that the enemies are so frequently described as deceivers, using treachery, falsehood, flattery and whispering. They are wild beasts lurking in secret, waiting to pounce unexpectedly on their prey. Evil places unseen hazards in people's path, causing them to stumble and fall towards the realm of death. It is 'something dark, uncanny that shuns light'.[20] It functions by stealth, and is frequently associated with deceitful words (5:6; 28:3; 64:2; 109:2). It is by their lying, flattering or whispering words that the workers of evil (*pō'ªlê 'āwen*) lead people astray.

More subtly still, it works through seduction. The special power of evil lies in the fact that it is enticing, and so attracts people towards it unawares. This is implied in the word 'snare', which can stand for the allurement posed, for example, for the Israelite people by the idol worship of the surrounding peoples. Evil is the seducer, a force outside human beings which entices them into evil ways by stealth and cunning. It follows from this that humans are not themselves the source of evil, but the victims of a seductive force which cuts them off from God. Deceived and seduced, humans are drawn by evil away from God and life, into the desolate territory of God-forsakenness and death.

Evil in the Heart

What happens when people are deceived and seduced in this way? How in practice does this independent, hostile force of evil affect human life? Wicked behaviour arises because evil operates by a special process, namely by lodging in the heart. The heart, in Hebrew thought, was a person's inmost being, the seat and source of the inner life. The thought of evil in the heart is one which occurs most of all in the book of Jeremiah (3:17, RSV; 4:14, 18; 7:24, RSV), but it is found also in the Psalms. The workers of evil are those

> who speak peace with their neighbours,
>> while mischief [or 'evil', *rā'āh*] is in their hearts. (28:3)

or

> who plan evil things in their minds [or 'heart', *lēb*] (140:2)

So the psalmist can pray to be protected from the evil that would take over his heart:

> Do not turn my heart to any evil. (141:4)

Indeed it is possible for evil to be 'cherished' in the heart in a way which separates a person from God:

> If I had cherished iniquity [*'āwen*] in my heart,
>> the Lord would not have listened. (66:18)

That is to say, evil produces within people an evil disposition, an attitude or inclination, and it is this that leads them to wicked behaviour and separates them from God. 'The power of a man,' comments Ricoeur, 'is mysteriously taken possession of by an inclination to evil that corrupts its very source.'[21] It is by lodging in a person's inner being that evil brings forth wicked deeds.

When evil enters people's hearts it leads not only to wicked deeds but also to disastrous consequences for the people themselves. While this may happen through God's punishment,[22] it is a common thought in the Psalms that evil brings its own nemesis. Those who, by allowing themselves to be caught up in evil, devise some harm for their neighbours, frequently find that the evil turns back on them (7:16). Augustine, commenting on 5:10 ('let them fall by their own counsels'), says that God punishes transgressors 'not by bringing evil upon them from himself, but by driving them on to what they have chosen'.[23] They plan hurt for others, but are hurt themselves. Those who dig a pit for others find that they fall into it themselves (7:15; 9:15; 57:6). They become ensnared in their own nets (35:8; 141:10). This happens because wicked deeds are an outworking of a power of evil in which they have become enmeshed, and which affects themselves as well as their victims.

This way of looking at evil leads to an important point about sin. The biblical view is often held to be that it was through human sinful actions that evil came into the world, and that human beings are therefore responsible for the existence of evil. Interpreting the Garden of Eden story, Eichrodt maintains that 'the cause of all evil, the reason for a distortion in the order of creation, was alienation from God' which resulted from human disobedience.[24] That is to say, evil has come about through human sin. Our interpretation of the imagery of the Psalms, however, suggests that the psalmists viewed it the other way round. It was not human disobedience which gave rise to evil, but the pre-existent power of evil which led to human sin. It is because evil exists as a mysterious force outside human beings, which seduces them, ensnares them and leads them away from God, that people commit sin. That is to say, it is evil that produces human sin. 'Sins' or 'transgressions' are another way of describing things which people do when they are affected or taken over by evil.[25]

In the Bible, human beings are indeed held responsible for their sinful deeds, so that it is necessary to repent and turn to God for forgiveness. But to say this gives no hint of the true reality and nature of evil. The real source of evil is not in humans but beyond them. In Ricoeur's words, 'The evil for which I assume responsibility makes manifest a source of evil for which I cannot assume responsibility, but which I participate in.'[26] Evil enters people, but it does so as a foreign body. It takes a person captive and corrupts, but 'it is not something that replaces the goodness of a man'.[27]

Therefore, in order to deal with evil it is indeed necessary for people to repent, but, in Levenson's words, 'more than just human repentance is necessary'.[28] The evil which is beyond human beings and which ensnares and leads them into sin cannot be dealt with only by human repentance. It requires the assertion of a greater or suprahuman power. It needs the intervention of God. That is why the psalmists cried to God for deliverance.

A Mystery

Our study has shown that psalms use a great variety of images to point to evil as a suprahuman power, hostile towards God and humans, which, in spite of God's victory and supreme power, continues to act with stealth and seduction to entice people into wicked deeds and thoughts, to separate the world and its people from God and draw them down to the realm of death and God-forsakenness. These images point beyond themselves to something transcendent, to a mystery which cannot be explained by processes of thought, or expounded in rational prose. Confronted by this mystery the psalmists can do nothing but cry out to God to be present and to deliver them. And perhaps it was the very vehemence and urgency of this cry that provides a clue to the question of the proper human response to evil, and to the nature of deliverance.

Chapter 9

Images of Deliverance: (1) God the Protector

We turn now from images which speak of evil and its dangers to those which tell of the power of God to deliver and protect from evil. The twin ideas of being delivered or saved and of being kept or protected are very prominent in the Psalms, and are expressed not only by a variety of images but also by a remarkably large number of general words, and it will be useful to look at some of these first. Some tell of deliverance, and some of protection, but a look at their use shows that they are very close in meaning.

Deliverance and Protection

There are no fewer than ten Hebrew words which are used to express the idea of being delivered or saved, and together they are found well over a hundred times in the Psalter.[1] Pleas or cries to God to deliver or save occur more than fifty times, very often taking the form of the simple imperative 'Deliver me!' or 'Save me!', which is the most common prayer in the whole book of Psalms. Sometimes the prayer is a very general one, without specifying what the danger is, especially when the word *y-š-ʿ*, 'to save', is used:

> O save your people, and bless your heritage. (28:9)

> Save your servant who trusts in you. (86:2)

But more usually the psalmists speak of deliverance from specific dangers, which are very often described in terms of the images of evil which we have considered in the previous chapters – deliverance from enemies or persecutors (31:15; 59:1 and frequently), from wild beasts (22:20–21), from snares and traps (91:3; 124:7), from many or deep waters (69:1, 14;

144:7) and from death or the power of Sheol (56:13; 89:48; 116:8). Salvation for the psalmists is, in Aubrey Johnson's words, 'liberation from the forces of evil which constantly threaten the life of the individual and of society at large.'[2] Deliverance is largely a matter of deliverance from evil in one form or another.

If God delivers, he also protects or keeps those whom he delivers. The common Hebrew verb *š-m-r*, and the less common *n-ṣ-r*, both meaning 'to keep, protect or guard', are sometimes used with much the same sense as the verbs rendered 'deliver':

> Protect me [*š-m-r*], O God, for in you I take refuge. (16:1)

> You, O LORD, will protect us [*š-m-r*];
> you will guard us [*n-ṣ-r*] from this generation for ever. (12:7)

In Ps. 140, words translated 'deliver' and 'protect' are used in close association:

> Deliver me, O LORD, from evildoers;
> protect me [*n-ṣ-r*] from those who are violent. (v. 1)

> Guard me [*š-m-r*], O LORD, from the hands of the wicked;
> protect [*n-ṣ-r*] me from the violent. (v. 4)

But *š-m-r* in particular can be used to express powerfully and emotively the additional sense that God cares for, watches over, and looks after his people; as, for example, in Ps. 121, which uses the word six times within as many verses, and in the unique: 'Guard me as the apple of the eye' (17:8). We are reminded that the idea of protection was present in the special blessing with which the priests blessed the people: 'The LORD bless you and keep you' (*š-m-r*, Num. 6:24). And, like the words for deliverance, those signifying protection can be used in connection with images of evil:

> Keep me [*š-m-r*] from the trap that they have laid for me,
> and from the snares of evildoers (141:9);

or they can refer directly to evil:

> The LORD will keep you [*š-m-r*] from all evil [*ra '*];
> he will keep your life. (121:7)

The frequency and use of all these words in the Psalter shows just how important it was to be delivered and kept from evil. For the psalmists,

God is both deliverer and protector: he both rescues them from evil and guards them against it. If we return now to the imagery of the Psalms we find this theme recurring, with particular emphasis on the idea of protection from evil. The images concerned may for convenience be divided into two groups, those which speak directly of God as deliverer or protector, and those which tell of being under God's protection. In this chapter we look at the first group, those which are directly images of God.

Shield and Buckler

The Psalms refer to two kinds of shields used in battle. The one spoken of most often, the *māgēn*, was a small round shield, normally covered with leather, held on a warrior's arm.[3] There was also a larger, longer shield, known as a *ṣinnāh*, which covered the whole body. In the large majority of cases (13 out of 19) where these words are used as metaphors or images, it is God himself who is said to be a shield:

> God is my shield,
>> who saves the upright in heart. (7:10)

> He is a shield for all who take refuge in him. (18:30)

> The LORD is my strength and my shield. (28:7)

> You are my hiding-place and my shield. (119:114)

Elsewhere God is said to use a shield:

> Take hold of shield and buckler [*māgēn* and *ṣinnāh*]
>> and rise up to help me! (35:2)

Or it is God's favour (5:12) salvation (18:35) or faithfulness (91:4) that is the shield.

In two places it appears to be the king, God's anointed, who is described a shield:

> Behold our shield, O God;
>> look on the face of your anointed. (84:9)

> For our shield belongs to the LORD,
>> our king to the Holy One of Israel. (89:18)

In each of these cases there is an alternative translation in which God is the shield.[4] But even in the version quoted here it is clear that the king is a shield for his people only because he depends on God. The king is 'the one who mediates to them God's protection from evil'.[5] In all instances it is ultimately God who is the shield.

The image is, of course, one of battle, of warriors defending themselves against attack. In many cases it occurs in psalms which speak of 'enemies' or 'the wicked', who, as we saw in Chapter 5, represent the forces of evil. Just as the 'enemies' should not be regarded literally as hostile armies, so the 'shield' is not literally a piece of a soldier's armour, but an image used very generally to describe God's protection. When the psalmists address God as 'a shield around me' (3:3); and 'my shield in whom I take refuge' (144:2), they have clearly moved away from the thought of the physical object, and are using the word as a general metaphor. A shield can be thought of as surrounding, 'hedging around'[6] or 'enveloping'[7] as in the words of Ps. 5, 'You cover [literally 'surround'] them with favour as with a shield [*ṣinnāh*]' (5:12). Jewish interpreters regarded the *māgēn* as a shield which protected from three sides, and the *ṣinnāh* as 'encircling armour' which added protection to the fourth.[8]

The image of a shield thus speaks of God as protector in a very general way. It seems to have been an ancient description or title for God[9] (see Gen. 15:1; Deut. 33:29). The repetition of the phrase 'He is our [or their] help and shield' in 33:20 and 115:9, 10, 11, suggests that it may have been a stereotyped cultic affirmation, perhaps used antiphonally within the temple cult.[10] It is an image which represents one of the basic Israelite beliefs about God, that he is a protector. He was their 'shield of salvation' (18:35), or 'saving shield', that is, one who protects his people.

It is interesting that other parts of a soldier's armoury are not used as images of this kind. There may be a reference to a soldier's helmet in 140:7:

> O LORD, my Lord, my strong deliverer,
>   you have covered my head in the day of battle,

but perhaps we should see this instead simply as a moving general metaphor for the deeply personal and intimate protection against evil which God provides. More important is the fact that in the Psalms weapons of attack are never used as images of God. Occasionally God is said to use arrows (7:13; 18:14; 64:7; 144:6), a spear (35:3) or a sword (7:12; 17:13) against the wicked, but nowhere is God referred to as our sword, our spear, our bow or our arrows. There is little suggestion that the psalmists felt that they had to go out and fight the enemy or forces of evil, the most obvious exceptions being Pss 18 and 149. God was their shield, not their sword, their defence and protection from evil powers, not their inspiration to attack.

Refuge and Rock

The theme of refuge is a very common one in the Psalms, and is represented in a number of ways. The verb 'to take refuge' is usually put in the mouth of an individual, frequently at the very beginning of a psalm, and is often connected with a plea for deliverance:

> Protect me, O God, for in you I take refuge. (16:1)

> In you, O LORD, I seek refuge;
>> do not let me ever be put to shame;
>> in your righteousness deliver me. (31:1; see also 7:1; 18:2; 57:1; 71:1; 144:2)

In addition there is a large number of nouns which indicate places where someone in danger could find safety, protection and security. One of the most common, *maḥseh*, is a word referring to a refuge or shelter in a general way, but there is also 'fortress', meaning a mountain fastness or stronghold in the wilderness; 'stronghold', referring to something high, and therefore a secure height; 'tower', meaning a watch-tower in a fortified city; and words with the broad meaning of 'refuge' which denote more specifically a place of safety, a shelter or booth, a dwelling place or habitation, a means of escape, and a hiding place.

Taken literally, all of these refer to places, either natural or constructed, which provide defence against enemy attack or shelter from the elements. But all of them are used figuratively to refer to the protection given by God. It is God who is the place of refuge. The word for a 'hiding place' (*sēter*, 32:7; 119:114, often translated 'shelter', 61:4; 91:1), in particular, points to a place provided by God in which one can hide oneself, or in which one is hidden by God himself:

> For he will hide me in his shelter [or 'hiding place']
>> in the day of trouble. (27:5)

> In the shelter [or 'hiding place'] of your presence you hide them
>> from human plots. (31:20)

The variety and frequency of these words make it clear that the sense of God as a place of refuge was very important for the psalmists. Sometimes a number of them are bunched together, along with images of danger and evil and other images of protection, to emphasise the sheer necessity of God's deliverance and protection (see especially 18:1–5; 31:1–4; 91:1–4).

A more specific image is that of the rock, which is often found alongside references to places of refuge. In this metaphor, represented by two synonymous Hebrew words, we have a flexible and varied image, found throughout the Old Testament, and quite frequently in the Psalms. It is a strong and important image, occurring most of all in the psalms of the individual, where God is quite frequently addressed personally as 'my rock' (in 18:2 twice, using both Hebrew words, and on eight other occasions). The rock is seen as a defence or protection against dangers of various kinds, which are often described by means of some of the images of evil with which we are now familiar.

The danger comes in some cases from 'enemies'. 'Rock' can be used in parallel with 'fortress' or 'stronghold', suggesting scenes of battle, with or without direct reference to enemies:

> Be a rock of refuge for me,
>   a strong fortress to save me.
> You are indeed my rock and my fortress. (31:2–3)

> Lead me to the rock
>   that is higher than I;
> for you are my refuge,
>   a strong tower against the enemy. (61:2–3)

> Blessed be the LORD, my rock,
>   who trains my hands for war, and my fingers for battle;
> my rock and my fortress,
>   my stronghold and my deliverer. (144:1–2)

In these cases a rock is envisaged as a very large strong object which can be used as a fort or a tower – possibly something behind which warriors took cover, or in front of which they took a stand. 'A soldier warding off a frontal attack,' explains an early Jewish commentator, 'may stand with his back against a rock to protect him against attack from behind.'[11] The rock is a protection against evil in the form of enemy attack.

Alternatively, the rock may be something firm and secure under one's feet. When there is danger of being overwhelmed by floods or of sinking in deep mire, one needs a steady rock on which to stand. A rock is thus a protection against the threat of being dragged down by evil into the realm of the underworld and death. So when the poet of Ps. 40 recalls how God rescued him:

> He drew me up from the desolate pit,
>   out of the miry bog,
> and set my feet upon a rock,
>   making my steps secure, (40:2)

the rock is for him 'a symbol of security and safety in contrast to the miry bog of the underworld.'[12] Similarly, when the psalmist of Ps. 42, feeling the waves and billows going over him, calls out to 'God my rock' (vv. 7, 9), there is 'an implicit contrast to the mire and waters of the underworld.'[13] Just as the sea represented the threat of evil and death, so the rock was a means of escape from this threat.[14] 'Only Yhwh the rock,' says Keel citing 18:2; 28:1 and 40:2, 'is able to provide a sure foundation' in 'the miry . . . realm of the dead.'[15]

But the rock may also stand for something of a different kind. According to a tradition which may have gone back to pre-Israelite times,[16] the temple in Jerusalem was built on what was regarded as a sacred rock. It was this that made Jerusalem secure and firm. One of the features of Mount Zion on whose rock the temple was built was that it could not 'be moved' (46:5; 125:1). Although the powers of evil attempted to shake the world and its people and cause them to 'be moved' (see pp. 77f), they could not prevail. When psalmists spoke of the rock there may have been a hidden reference to the temple. In Ps. 27 the 'rock' is mentioned in parallel with the 'tent' or 'tabernacle', which was the archaic name for the temple:

> He will conceal me under the cover of his tent;
>   he will set me high on a rock. (27:5)

The rock, then, was something immovable like the temple on Mount Zion which could not be overcome by evil. To call God a rock was to declare one's trust in him as an unshakable and reliable protection against its assaults.

But although the image of the rock can be linked in this way to images of battle, of deep waters or of the temple, there are occasions when it is used apparently without any specific reference. Sometimes, as in 27:5, protection from a storm may be in mind; but at other times God is simply spoken of as a rock, almost as a name or a title. The metaphor seems to have become a very general one, signifying that God was a source of protection and security.

> To you, O LORD, I call;
>> my rock, do not refuse to hear me. (28:1)

> They remembered that God was their rock,
>> the Most High God their redeemer. (78:35)

> He is my rock, and there is no unrighteousness in him. (92:15)

In these contexts the emphasis is entirely on God: it is he who is the rock. Faced with the threat of evil the psalmists are aware that they cannot rely on their own strength for security: their protection comes entirely from God.

> My flesh and my heart may fail,
>> but God is the rock [NRSV 'strength'] of my heart
>> and my portion forever. (73:26)

This rock is 'higher than I', or 'too high for me' (61:2). It is a 'place of deliverance the singer of the lament is no longer able to reach under his own power',[17] since 'when a man finds himself in extreme trouble, it is only God who can bring him to safety.'[18] As in the case of the shield, the emphasis is not so much on the character of the rock, as on the fact that it is God alone who provides the security and protection.

The Shadow of Your Wings

The image of the shadow or shelter of God's wings may seem a surprising one to find in a religious tradition which rejects any representation of God in animal form. But it is a significant image, as it represents an aspect of God's protection not found in others. The phrase 'shadow of your wings' is found four times in the Psalter:

> Hide me in the shadow of your wings. (17:8)

> All people may take refuge in the shadow of your wings. (36:7)

> In the shadow of your wings I will take refuge. (57:1)

> In the shadow of your wings I sing for joy. (63:7)

In addition we have 'the shelter of your wings' (61:4), and 91:4 also refers to God's pinions and wings. There are two principal ways in which the phrase can be interpreted, and it is not necessary to choose exclusively between them.[19]

The most obvious way is to see the shadow of God's wings as a metaphor of a bird gathering her young under her wings for protection. The Hebrew word *ṣēl* ('shadow' or 'shade') has none of the negative connotations which 'shadow' can have in the English of the western world, but is a positive word frequently meaning shade from the burning heat of the sun. In the sense of shadow it is an expression for an immediate area of protection, so that a king's subjects can be said to live 'under his shadow',[20] and God himself can be described as 'your shade at your right hand' (121:5). To be in the shadow of God's wings, therefore, is to be under his close protection, like fledgling birds in the watchful care of the mother bird. The image is a powerful and moving one, as is shown by its repetition on the lips of Jesus:

> 'Jerusalem, Jerusalem . . . How often have I desired to gather your children together as a hen gathers her brood under her wings, and you were not willing!' (Luke 13:34)

And it is further reinforced by the use of the figure of wings elsewhere in the Bible to speak in a somewhat different way of God's care for his people:

> You have seen what I did to the Egyptians, and how I bore you on eagles' wings and brought you to myself. (Exod. 19:4)

> As an eagle stirs up its nest,
>   and hovers over its young;
> as it spreads its wings, takes them up,
>   and bears them aloft on its pinions,
> the LORD alone guided him. (Deut. 32:11–12)

Seen in this way, the image speaks not only of protection from danger, but also of tenderness and care, as of a bird for its young, and adds a further dimension to what it means to be kept by God.

But it can also be interpreted in a different way. The wings may refer not to those of a mother bird but to the wings of the cherubim which covered the ark of the covenant in the temple. Carved figures of these strange winged creatures were poised over the ark, spreading their wings over the 'mercy-seat', the supreme symbol of God's presence, and covering it with the 'shadow of their wings' (see Exod. 25:17–20). The image may then refer to the protective presence of God in the temple; and to take refuge or hide in the shadow of God's wings would be to find security in this presence.[21] Seen in this way it recalls the imagery of the two realms, of God and of evil, and of the temple as the place of God's presence at the heart of his realm, where people could dwell and find their safety from the powers of evil.

Whether we understand the wings to be those of a mother bird or those of the cherubim in the temple – and both these references, and perhaps others, may be present – the image speaks powerfully of God's protection, given with tender care and given through his presence in the sanctuary. It is also worth noting briefly that it is linked in one place with another beautiful metaphor, mentioned earlier:

> Guard [or 'keep', š-m-r] me as the apple of the eye,
>   hide me in the shadow of your wings. (17:8)

The image of the 'apple of the eye' is found only here, in Prov. 7:2 and in Deut. 32:10 where it is followed immediately by the metaphor of the eagle's wings quoted above.[22] It refers to the pupil of the eye, and is 'an emblem of that which is tenderest and dearest, and therefore guarded with the most jealous care'.[23] Taken together with the image of the shadow of God's wings it adds something more to the feeling of the tenderness and carefulness of God's protection.

God Our Portion

Another image which is more significant than the frequency of its occurrence might indicate is that of God as 'my portion', found in 16:5; 73:26; 119:57; and 142:5. The Hebrew word *ḥēleq* means generally 'a share', or something allocated, but it is used with special reference to the division of the land of Canaan amongst the tribes of Israel, in which each received its portion or inheritance, to be the source of their life (Josh. 18–19). The priestly tribe of Levi, however, was not given a portion of land, because Yhwh himself was to be their inheritance (Deut. 10:9; Num. 18:20). God alone was to be the basis of their life, and they were to derive their livelihood from the temple and the work of the priesthood (Josh. 18:7; Deut. 18:1–2).

It is in this context that the references to God as 'my portion' should be understood. Ps. 16 in particular, where 'drink-offerings' (v. 4) and 'my cup' (v. 5) suggest temple rituals, may have the situation of the Levites in mind:

> The LORD is my chosen [or 'allotted'] portion and my cup;
>   you hold my lot. (16:5)

Here the psalmist implies that just as the Levites had God himself as their inheritance and the basis of their life, so, by a process of spiritualising the situation of the Levites, the LORD could be the portion for others too, the single thing to be depended on for their life. When they prayed 'You are my portion', they were 'making the prerogative of the Levites their own'.[24] The word could then be used by anyone, to tell of their total devotion to and dependence on God, as when Ps. 119 says simply 'The LORD is my portion' (119:57). But it may have been used especially by those people who had no worldly inheritance of their own, those 'who no longer had the right to exist in "the land of the living"', 'those threatened with loss of life, the sick and those marked for death'.[25] For such people the LORD was in a special way their portion or inheritance, the one thing they could be sure of. The association with the allocation of land could also be a reminder that they belonged in God's territory, the realm of God that is opposed to the realm of evil and death. Without worldly security, they nevertheless had their 'portion in the land of the living' (142:5), their own allocated place in the sphere of life (cf Isa. 57:13).

The portion, then, is the basis of one's life and thus one's source of security. So Ps. 16 (quoted above) which speaks of God as 'my portion' begins with the thought of God as refuge:

> Protect me, O God, for in you I take refuge.
> I say to the LORD, 'You are my Lord;
>   I have no good apart from you.' (16:1–2)

And Ps. 142 places portion and refuge together:

> You are my refuge, my portion in the land of the living. (142:5)

The refuge in this case has a special characteristic. Since it is one's portion it is something allocated, a permanent heritage which supplies one's livelihood, and so it cannot be taken away. The security given by God, like the Levites' portion, is inalienable. The portion is thus a symbol of deep confidence in the protection of God in all circumstances of life.

It is an essential aspect of this image, as of the previous ones, that the portion consists ultimately of God himself. Unlike the inheritance of the other tribes which was a piece of land, the portion of the Levites, although it included the duties and the income of the temple, was essentially not something owned or possessed, but was simply 'the LORD'. The use of the image in the Psalms expresses this truth for anyone, in a deeply personal way: 'The LORD is *my* portion'. Ultimate security and permanent protection for the individual person is not anything which God gives, but is simply God himself.

Chapter 10

Images of Deliverance: (2) Under God's Protection

Having looked at images of God as protector, we turn now to some others which suggest ways in which God delivers and protects, or which say something about what it is like to be under God's protection. A first group of these has to do with being in God's place or space, and a second with the nearness and presence of God.

A Place of Safety

The idea that God gives room or space is found in several psalms. A form of the Hebrew verb *r-ḥ-b* meaning 'to enlarge' or 'to give room', together with the cognate noun *merḥāb*, 'a broad place', is used to describe the experience of being delivered:

> Answer me when I call, O God of my right!
>> You gave me room when I was in distress. (4:1)

A literal translation of this last line – 'In distress you gave me room' – brings out the contrast between being in distress and being in a roomy place. The noun for distress is the common word *ṣar* meaning straits, narrowness or restriction (see p. 31). To be in *ṣar* was to be in 'a tight, constricted place';[1] while to be delivered was to be brought out of such a place into a broad area of openness and freedom. Sometimes the broad place and deliverance are explicitly linked together:

> He brought me out into a broad place [*merḥāb*];
>> he delivered me, because he delighted in me. (18:19)

'In the Hebrew idiom,' says Anderson, '"distress" is a condition of being hemmed in by trouble, while "deliverance" is to be brought out of affliction, out of the stranglehold of distress, into a broad place, to be set at liberty.'² So the poet of Ps. 25 can pray to God to 'Relieve the troubles [plural of *ṣar*] of my heart,' or, 'make wide the narrow places of my heart' (25:17).³

The connection between deliverance and being given room may be further hinted at by the use of the common word *y-š-ʿ*, to save. While it is hazardous to take the meaning of words from their etymology,⁴ it does appear that the root idea of 'being wide' still lingers in this word.⁵ It seems that the plea to God to 'Save me', found frequently in the psalms of the individual, may have within it a desire to be brought out of straits into a roomy place.

This idea of room or space also carries with it the sense of freedom. It contrasts both with the straits of distress, and also with the sense of imprisonment or being shut in which was mentioned in Chapter 7 (see pp. 78ff). It 'is a concept of "nomadic feeling for life" (Gen. 26:22) that sees the expanse and the liberty of unrestricted possibilities before it'.⁶ It expresses the feeling of 'free space for unobstructed movement'.⁷ This idea of freedom of movement is conveyed especially by some verses where the broad place is related to 'feet' or 'steps':

> You gave me a wide place for my steps under me,
>   and my feet did not slip. (18:36)

> [You] have not delivered me into the hand of the enemy;
>   you have set my feet in a broad place [*merḥāb*] (31:8)

To have one's feet in a broad place is to be able to move freely, as is stressed by a paraphrase of this verse offered by Ibn Ezra, a famous medieval Jewish scholar, 'You have . . . widened my stride. I enjoyed complete freedom of movement.'⁸

The idea of being able to walk or move freely is found also in the metaphor of a level path. Just as the threat of evil could be expressed in terms of the fear of stumbling or falling on a steep rocky path (see pp. 75ff), so the idea of safety or protection could be expressed by the image of a level or even path, that is, a path unencumbered by rocks or hindrances:

> Lead me on a level path because of my enemies. (27:11)⁹

> Let your good spirit lead me on a level path. (143:10)¹⁰

The word 'level' (literally 'levelness') can be used on its own to describe ground that is plain and even, as in 26:12, 'My foot stands on level ground', or in the familiar words of Deutero-Isaiah, 'The uneven ground shall become level' (Isa. 40:4), where the 'uneven ground' refers to steep mountainous terrain. The level path is 'a path along a level open plain, free from pitfalls and places where enemies may lurk in ambush,'[11] and so it is an image of safety.[12] The level path or ground is to be contrasted with the uneven, rocky path where one's feet may stumble and fall. Those who keep to God's paths are able to say:

> My steps have held fast to your paths;
> > my feet have not slipped. (17:5)

Because they are on smooth level ground they will not fall into the realm of death, but will remain on the 'path of life' (16:11).

Both these images, that of the broad place and that of the level path, have to do with ground or territory, and so remind us of the image of God's realm or territory, which we discussed in Chapter 7. God's country, the sphere or realm of God which stands in opposition to the realm of evil, is a place of breadth, spaciousness, smoothness and freedom into which God leads his people, and in which they can walk in safety on a level path. This realm, symbolised by the temple, God's 'house' built on the 'holy hill' of Zion, is the special place of safety and protection. To dwell in this safe place, protected from the assaults of evil and the encroachments of the realm of death, is the earnest desire of God's people:

> One thing I asked of the LORD,
> > that will I seek after;
> to live in the house of the LORD
> > all the days of my life . . .
> For he will hide me in his shelter
> > in the day of trouble. (27:4–5)

> And I shall dwell in the house of the LORD
> > my whole life long. (23:6).

Or, in other words, they long for God to lead them to this place of safety. The frequently reiterated prayer to be 'led' is not so much a plea for guidance or instruction about how to live, as a prayer to be given security and refuge by being led into the sphere of God:[13]

> O send out your light and your truth;
> > let them lead me;
> let them bring me to your holy hill
> > and to your dwelling. (43:3; see also 5:8; 31:3; 61:2; 143:10)

This then is one picture of how God delivers and protects his people: he leads them into his own realm, bringing them into a broad place of freedom, making their feet secure on level ground, and causing them to dwell in safety.

God's Presence

The temple was important largely because it was the place where, in a special way, God was felt to be present. We have seen that presence was expressed in Hebrew by the word *pānîm*, literally 'face'. Although God's presence was not confined to one place, devout people went to the temple in order to 'seek' or 'behold God's face', to have a special sense of his presence (11:7; 17:15; 27:8; 42:2; 105:4). It was the presence of God which gave shelter and protection. So it can be said of those who take refuge in God,

> In the shelter [or 'hiding place'] of your presence [*pānîm*] you hide
> them from human plots;
> you hold them safe under your shelter [or 'booth']
> from contentious tongues. (31:20)

God's presence constitutes the hiding place or sheltering booth in which God the protector hides his own from the devious schemes and malicious words which are the weapons of evil.

We saw earlier that God could at times be said to 'hide his face', to withdraw his presence, bringing dismay and possible disaster. By contrast, there were other occasions when he 'caused his face to shine' (see 119:135). This was a 'picturesque description of a favourable attitude',[14] and 'a sign of the gracious and friendly presence of God'.[15] The shining of God's face brought blessing and goodness:

> My God be gracious to us and bless us
> and make his face to shine upon us. (67:1)

And so the priests of Israel blessed the people with the words:

> The LORD bless you and keep you;
> the LORD make his face to shine upon you. (Num. 6:24–25)

This image could, however, speak not only of blessing but also of protection. It was by causing his face to shine that God saved and delivered his people:

> Let your face shine upon your servant;
> save me in your steadfast love (31:16)

a thought emphasised particularly in Ps. 80 with its twice repeated refrain:

> Restore us, O God;
> > let your face shine, that we may be saved. (80:3, 7, 19).

God delivered not by some physical power or force of arms, but simply by his presence.

The idea of God's presence, which is given graphic expression by the metaphor of God's face, can be given less figurative expression by the idea of God being 'with us'. This is a common and important phrase in other parts of the Bible, but it is not found often in the Psalms, perhaps because the psalmists preferred more figurative expressions. The principal exceptions are the familiar words of Ps. 23:

> Even though I walk through the valley of the shadow of death,[16]
> > I fear no evil [*ra'*];
> for you are with me;
> > your rod and your staff –
> > they comfort me (23:4)

and the similar sentiment of Ps. 46:

> Therefore we will not fear, though the earth should change . . .
> The LORD of hosts is with us;
> > the God of Jacob is our refuge. (46:2, 7; see also 91:15)

Here again, as with the metaphor of God's face, it is by being 'with' his people that God delivers and protects.

Another way of referring to the presence of God is to say that he is near. Just as the sense that God was far from them was a cause of distress to the psalmists (see pp. 72ff), so the sense of his being near brought relief and comfort. Although he was believed to be near to the whole people of Israel (148:14) especially through his presence in the temple,[17] he was in a special way near to those individuals who feared and called upon him.

> The LORD is near to all who call on him,
> > to all who call on him in truth.
> He fulfils the desire of all who fear him;
> > he also hears their cry, and saves them. (145:18–19)

There is, moreover, a particularly close connection between 'being near' and 'saving', as can be seen from the use of the two ideas in parallel:

> The LORD is near to the broken-hearted,
> > and saves the crushed in spirit.

> Many are the afflictions of the righteous,
>> but the LORD rescues them from them all. (34:18–19)

Elsewhere it is the presence of enemies or persecutors, the agents of evil, and the need to be delivered from them, which make God's nearness necessary:

> Draw near to me, redeem me,
>> set me free because of my enemies. (69:18)

> Those who persecute me with evil purpose draw near;
>> they are far from your law.
> Yet you are near, O LORD. (119:150–151)

It is simply by being near, not by any special action, that God delivers. The nearness of God itself is deliverance and protection.[18] Indeed God's nearness is not just a comforting presence, but an active power to rescue or save. 'The nearness of God is never anything static . . . but a movement emanating from God, who intervenes on earth and demonstrates his liberating, salutary presence.'[19]

God our Deliverance and Protection

The main point, therefore, which emerges from these images of deliverance is once again that it is God himself who is the deliverance and protection. Simply by being present he gave his people security. When the psalmists called on God to deliver or save them, they were not asking primarily for an act of God or an assertion of his power, but for his presence. They were delivered precisely by his being there, or being near. God's presence and nearness was not only in itself the greatest good, but also the means by which people could be rescued and protected from evil.

The power of God to deliver was of a completely different nature from the hostile power of evil. When we saw earlier that evil was felt to be a suprahuman, objective reality, a mysterious power which could not be explained rationally but could be represented only by image and myth, we observed that this power was not seen as a personal being, i.e. a 'Devil', but as a mysterious impersonal force (see p. 85). We see now that against it is set, not some countervailing impersonal power, but simply a personal presence, the living reality of the personal God. God is not just the Deliverer: he is Deliverance itself. He is not just the Protector: he is Protection itself.

We can understand this statement if we recall that the principal character of evil was hostility to God. In the symbolic form of enemies or of the deep waters of chaos it sought to disrupt God's order. Its main aim in relation to human beings was to separate them from God, by means of the attacks of enemies, or the overwhelming power of the great waters and primeval chaos, or by causing them to slip from God's domain and dragging them into the domain of death. It used all kinds of deceitful means to draw or seduce them away from God. Its object was God-forsakenness, a state in which people were cut off from the source of life. It follows from this that if God were present, evil could not achieve its object. Simply to be near God, to be with him or in his realm, was itself deliverance. For the frustration of evil all that was necessary was to be in his presence.

That is why the images of deliverance and protection that we looked at in the previous chapter focused simply on God himself. For the psalmists it was God alone who was their shield against the attacks of evil. He was the rock which provided shelter, or which prevented them from sinking in the waters of chaos. Under his protecting wings they were secure. He himself was their portion or lot, providing the basis of life and their source of security. It was the shining of his face and the light of his countenance, powerful symbols of his benevolent presence, that lifted them out of dismay and failure. In his realm or territory they found room to move in safety and freedom, and their feet did not slip. When evil sought to drag them down to death, the final separation, or to cause death and Sheol to encroach on them in the form of many ills and troubles, it was the living presence of God which was the only comfort and safety. So we have the repeated phrases: God is our shield, he is our rock, he is our portion, he is or refuge, he is our salvation.

The point may be illustrated by quoting again from Ps. 46:

> God is our refuge and strength,
>   a *very present* help in trouble . . .
> There is a river whose streams make glad the city of God,
>   the holy habitation of the Most High.
> God *is in the midst* of the city; it shall not be moved . . .
> The LORD of hosts is *with us*;
>   the God of Jacob is our refuge. (46:1, 4, 5, 7)

The whole point of this psalm which celebrates the security of the city is to emphasise the fact that it is God himself and nothing else that provides that security, and that he does so by his presence in the midst of it.[20] Its protection comes about because he is 'very present'.[21] It is because 'he is in the midst of the city' that 'it shall not be moved'. Their refuge consists simply of the fact that he is 'with us'.

Deliverance from Death

But if God gives deliverance and protection through his presence, what of death? Can God give the ultimate security, security from death? It is generally accepted that in most of the Old Testament there is no clear sign of a belief in life after death, or resurrection from the dead. When people died they went down to Sheol, the place of the dead, from which there was no return. This fate awaited all and was inescapable:

> Who can live and never see death?
>> Who can escape the power of Sheol? (89:48)

Moreover, Sheol was understood to be a place of separation from God. There people had no contact with God; they did not remember him, nor could they praise him:

> For in death there is no remembrance of you;
>> in Sheol who can give you praise? (6:5)

> Is your steadfast love declared in the grave,
>> or your faithfulness in Abaddon?
> Are your wonders known in the darkness,
>> or your saving help in the land of forgetfulness? (88:11–12)

> The dead do not praise the LORD,
>> nor do any that go down into silence. (115:17)

These statements could not be clearer: those who wrote them expected to be separated and cut off from God after death. Some could even use the fact that in Sheol they would not be able to praise God as a kind of bargaining counter to persuade God to save them from their impending death:

> What profit is there in my death,
>> if I go down to the Pit?
> Will the dust praise you?
>> Will it tell of your faithfulness? (30:9)

Death was for the individual an inescapable separation from God. It would appear then that evil has the final say. If it is the purpose and thrust of evil to cut people off from God, the inevitability of their descent into Sheol would seem to be the ultimate triumph of evil, at least as far as the individual is concerned. Faced with death, the individual has no unshakeable security.

There is in the Psalms no clear answer to this dilemma. But the psalmists do have other things to say about death. In the first place it is clear that when people were in danger of dying God could reverse events, and prevent them from going down to death:

> You are the one who lifts me up from the gates of death. (9:13)

> You do not give me up to Sheol,
>   or let your faithful one see the Pit. (16:10)

> The LORD has punished me severely,
>   but he did not give me over to death. (118:18)

That is to say, the power of evil to drag people down to death was not always irresistible. But the Psalms go further than this: they claim that God can deliver or rescue people from death.

> For you have delivered my soul from death,
>   and my feet from falling,
> so that I may walk before God
>   in the light of life. (56:13)

> You have delivered my soul from the depths of Sheol. (86:13; see
>   also 33:19; 116:3)

> O LORD, you brought up my soul from Sheol,
>   restored me to life from among those gone down to the Pit. (30:3)

What precisely is meant by delivering people from death or Sheol is not clear. Since, as we have seen, death was believed to encroach upon life in the form of illness and suffering, to be delivered from it may mean no more than to be relieved of suffering and saved from dying. But it does suggest at least that God is stronger than death; that he is able to take people out of the grip of death:

> Our God is a God of salvation,
>   and to GOD, the Lord, belongs escape from death. (68:20; cf 18:4)

There may even be a suggestion that God can raise people out of Sheol after they have died. A puzzling verse in Ps. 49 has been taken by some to indicate the psalmist's belief that God would 'receive' or 'take' him out of Sheol into a new life after death:

> But God will ransom my soul from the power of Sheol,
>   for he will receive [or 'take'] me. (49:15)

A similar belief is often thought to underlie the words of 73:24:

> You guide me with your counsel,
>> and afterwards you will receive me with honour [or 'to glory'],

where the same word 'receive' is used.[22] But perhaps more significant are the words of Ps 139:

> If I ascend to heaven, you are there;
>> if I make by bed in Sheol, you are there. (139:8)

In contrast with other statements quoted above, the psalmist here believes that God is indeed present in Sheol; that even death does not cut people off from him. A verse in Ps. 22 also suggests that, contrary to what is said elsewhere, those who have died may still praise God:

> To him, indeed, shall all who sleep in the earth bow down;
>> before him shall bow down all who go down to the dust. (22:29)[23]

It is apparent, then, that the Psalms say a number of different and some-times contradictory things about death. There is no clear or consistent theology. The reason for this may be in part that the psalmists simply did not ask the question about life after death. What would happen after death remained a mystery, something that could not be known, and about which speculation was useless. The important thing, however, was the presence of God. To be with God was all that anyone could need or desire. If death, or the suffering which was a form of death in the midst of life, threatened to separate people from God, their response was not to develop a faith in a resurrection from the dead, but simply to call out to God to be with them and not to withdraw his presence, and to trust in a communion with God which could not be destroyed. Even in death God remained their 'keeper'.[24] Some may have reached the conviction that God would raise them from the dead; but for many it was sufficient to seek and call for the presence of God now, in the belief that if God was with them they needed nothing else. In the words of Luther's paraphrase of 73:25, 'as long as I have thee, I wish for nothing else in heaven or on earth'.[25]

Securing God's Protection

One final question remains: if God's protection is simply God's presence; how does one avail oneself of this protection? It will be recalled that evil, although something suprahuman existing outside people, nevertheless found its way into them by way of the heart. Similarly, although it is simply God himself who is the deliverance and protection of his people, it is through the heart that this protection becomes a reality for them. The heart is the inner person, the seat of all thoughts and feelings. In itself the heart is neutral: it can be made to incline towards good or evil (119:36, 112; 141:4). It is possible to have a heart which 'cherishes iniquity' (66:18) or to have a 'double heart' (12:2), which is 'not steadfast' (78:8, 37). But it also possible to seek God or give thanks to him with one's 'whole heart' (9:1; 111:1; 119:2, 10; 138:1), that is, a heart which is not divided in its loyalty and love. So one psalmist can pray:

> Give me an undivided heart to revere your name.
> I give thanks to you, O Lord my God, with my whole heart.
> (86:11–12)[26]

Such a heart can also be described as 'clean' (51:10) or 'pure' (24:4; 73:1), the latter word meaning not ritually or morally pure, but clear and clean, not cluttered and encumbered, and so able to give full space and loyalty to God.[27] It is those who have a pure heart who are able to stand in God's holy place; who are able, that is, to come into his presence and discover his deliverance and protection:

> Who shall ascend the hill of the LORD?
>   And who shall stand in his holy place?
> Those who have clean hands and pure hearts. (24:3–4)

That is to say, God's deliverance and protection are made effective through the heart. It is by having a pure and undivided heart, open wholly to God, that a person can obtain the security that consists ultimately simply in God himself. It is when their hearts are firmly attached to God that people can face evil and the attacks of the enemies without fear:

> They are not afraid of evil tidings;
>   their hearts are firm, secure in the LORD,
> Their hearts are steady, they will not be afraid. (112:7–8)

One secures the deliverance and protection of God by directing one's heart and its desires wholly towards him.

This, however, does not supply the whole answer. The psalmists knew well that, even if one's heart was fixed on God, evil was still present and active in the world, and its attendant sufferings and woes still tormented both individuals and nations. Why this should be was a mystery, in the face of which the psalmists found themselves calling out 'Why?' (10:1; 22:1; 44:24; 74:11; 88:14). They were firm in their belief that God had overcome the powers of evil, but they could not understand why it still persisted. All they could do was to cry out to God to activate his powers, to come amongst them to remove the threat of evil. So we have the repeated earnest prayer of the individual 'Deliver me!', and the desperate cry of the people that the God who seemed to be doing nothing would rise up to deliver them:

> Rouse yourself! Why do you sleep, O Lord?
>> Awake, do not cast us off for ever! (44:23)

> Rise up, O God, plead your cause;
>> remember how the impious scoff at you all day long. (74:22)

The concern of the psalmists, as of most of the other biblical writers, was 'not to explain [evil] away but to call upon God to blast it away.'[28] Evil was a mysterious, inexplicable and unavoidable reality, finding expression in many forms but describable only through image and myth. The only answer to evil was the presence of God; and the only way to be delivered from evil was to cry out to him, and to seek that presence with their whole heart.

Chapter 11

Addressing God As Person

For the psalmists deliverance from evil came about simply through the presence of God. The meaning of this will become clearer if we turn now to the second feature on the Psalms mentioned in the first chapter, the fact they are addressed directly to God. We saw there that most of the psalms (104 out of 150) are addressed in whole or in part to God, and that in the large majority of these cases there is a movement between addressing God in the second person and speaking about him in the third. Sometimes there is a simple change from the second person to the third, as in Ps. 7:9–10, or from the third person to the second, as in Ps. 23:3–4. Sometimes one or two verses addressed to God occur suddenly and unexpectedly in the midst or at the end of a psalm which otherwise speaks of God in the third person (52:9; 93:5; 97:8–9; 135:13). Sometimes there is an oscillation, a to-ing and fro-ing between speaking to God and speaking about him (see especially Pss 18, 56, 94, 116, 145). This easy movement between talking about God and talking to him suggests that in these cases the whole of the psalm is uttered in God's presence and is in some way addressed to God. Whatever the precise grammatical form, God is present throughout in the mind of the speaker, and may at any time be turned to and addressed directly. The same may be said of all the psalms. There is no fundamental difference between second and third person speech. Sometimes a reference to God in the third person provides a lead in to a focus on him as 'you', as in Ps. 74, where the statement

> Yet God my King is from of old,
>> working salvation in the earth (v. 12)

is followed by five verses where the emphatic pronoun 'you' (*'attāh*) occurs six times.[1] Because of the limitations of thought and language humans have no choice but to think and speak of God in objective terms, as if he were not present, to speak *about* him as well as *to* him. But in his encounter with us God is always a subject, always another 'person' in whose presence we are. To speak of him as if he were a non-present object is always to some degree to falsify. In the words of Martin Buber, when we speak of God 'even "he" [or "she"] is a metaphor, while "you" is not'.[2] It is this that lies behind the psalmists' practice of alternating between direct address to God and speaking about him in the third person. While of necessity they often spoke of God in the third person, in doing so they remained aware of his presence, and switched every now and then to addressing him directly.

Personal Presence

The significance of this direct address is that it shows that for the psalmists God's presence was personal. Deliverance came about through the presence of one who could be addressed as a person. In the Old Testament generally but most of all in the Psalms, God is addressed as if he were a human person. He is often described, just as human beings are, in words which refer to parts of the human body. In many cases these are words which had become common metaphors in ordinary speech, such as 'face', 'hand', and 'arm'; but interestingly we also find reference to such features as God's 'fingers' (8:3), his 'bosom' (presumably of his garment, 74:11), and his 'form' (*t'mûnāh*, 17:15; cf. Num. 12:8). Emotions of a human type, such as anger, compassion, loathing, are also attributed to God. And throughout the Psalms the actions of God are described in human terms: God hears, laughs, whets his sword, shoots arrows, sleeps and wakes, sits enthroned, looks down at the earth, and so on. In other words, God is spoken of in unapologetically anthropomorphic terms, as if he were a human being. From this it should not be deduced that the psalmists had a primitive idea of God as a kind of being in human form, but rather that they were determined at all costs to preserve the sense of God as person, and were prepared to speak of him in human terms in order to emphasise his personal nature. As Buber has said, 'The concept of personhood is, of course, utterly incapable of describing the nature of God, but it is permitted and necessary to say that God is also a person'.[3] The psalmists preferred to risk the misunderstandings which could arise from their use of anthropomorphic language than to lose the sense of the personal nature of God which they could convey only by the use of this language. As von Rad says, with reference to the Old Testament as a whole:

For the people of the old covenant, Yhwh was completely
personal, a will most vital and lively. So far as the human
description of God is concerned (in terms of pleasure, anger,
aversion, zeal, love, etc.), the Old Testament (especially the
prophets) reveals scarcely any attempt to 'spiritualise' the picture
of God. It was apparently easier in Old Testament faith to tolerate
the danger of lessening God's greatness and 'absoluteness' by
human description than to run the risk of giving up anything of
God's lively personalness.[4]

This 'personalness' meant that God could be addressed as 'Thou' or
'You'. Most commonly this direct address was made in the first person
singular: there is an 'I' who addresses the 'Thou'. This is not always the
case: in some psalms it is 'we' or some unspecified wider group of
people who address God, (and we shall return to the significance of this
shortly); but it is the 'I' that stands out most clearly in the psalms of
direct address. It points to a very direct and personal 'I-Thou' or 'I-You'
relationship between the individual and God, an intimate relationship in
which the human person engages in dialogue with the personal God.

The psalmists were, of course, in no doubt about the transcendence of
God. He was great, holy, awesome; he had 'done marvellous things' and
was 'greatly to be praised'; he had made the heavens and the earth only
by the word of his mouth, and he sat enthroned in heaven looking down
on the earth and its inhabitants. He was to be worshipped with reverence
and prostrations. But this transcendent God was also immanent. And it is
important to note that this immanence had a special character. For the
psalmists it certainly meant that he was near (see p. 108 above), but,
more importantly, it meant also that he was a 'You', a personal presence
with whom a human being could enter a person-to-person relationship.
God's immanence consisted most of all in his 'You-ness', his presence
not as an object but as another subject.

The intimacy and personal nature of this relationship is emphasised by
the common use of the words 'My God'. This phrase occurs 54 times in
the Psalter, in a total of 34 psalms.[5] It is found most of all in psalms
usually classified as individual laments, in which the psalmist calls out to
God for deliverance and help:

Rise up, O LORD! Deliver me, O my God! (3:7)

My God, my God, why have you forsaken me?

> Why are you so far from helping me, from the words of my
> groaning?
> O my God, I cry by day, but you do not answer;
>   and by night, but find no rest. (22:1–2)

> O God, you are my God, I seek you,
>   my soul thirsts for you. (63:1)

But it occurs in other psalm types as well, including communal laments (83:13; 94:22), hymns (104:1; 145:1; 146:2), thanksgivings (18:6, 21, 28, 29; 30:12; 118:28), and others of various types (68:24; 84:3; 91:2; 119:115) including one which is clearly a royal psalm (89:26). The identity of the original speaker who addressed God in this personal way as 'My God' has been a subject of controversy. Some scholars who have held the view that a large proportion of the individual psalms were composed for recitation by the king during the rituals of festivals or on other occasions, have regarded the words 'my God' as a form of address used by the king in the context of the special relationship which existed between the king and Yhwh.[6] But it is clear from the occurrence of the phrase 'My God' in a wide variety of psalms, and from the use that has been made of these psalms throughout the centuries, that, whoever the original speaker may have been, any person of faith could address God as 'My God'. The important thing is not to discover who the original 'I' was, but to recognise that the words 'I' and 'My God' describe an intimate person-to-person relationship, in which the speaker acknowledges God to be a 'You', who can be addressed as a personal subject, and with whom there is an interpersonal dialogue.

Here it is worth noting in passing that whereas the psalmists habitually spoke to God directly as a person, they did not address their enemies in the same way. Although, as we have seen, the psalmists were aware of being surrounded by enemies, the wicked and evildoers, there is no dialogue with them. It is true that they are sometimes addressed, but the words spoken to them have the flavour of rhetorical devices, poetic forms of speech rather than words spoken directly to the wicked:

> Depart from me, all you workers of evil,
>   for the LORD has heard the sound of my weeping. (6:8)

> Why do you boast, O mighty one,
>   of mischief done against the godly? (52:1, see also vv. 2–5)

> Go away from me, you evildoers,
>   that I may keep the commandments of my God. (119:115)[7]

It is true that in a large number of psalms[8] the psalmists engage with the enemies in other ways, by drawing down curses or uttering imprecations against them. But this does not amount to a dialogue with enemies. In these cases the poet, instead of speaking directly to the enemies, stands aside from them to call on God to deal with them. For their part, the enemies are frequently said to address the psalmists, often seeking to provoke them with mocking words, especially the taunt of 'Where is your God?' (42:3, 10; 79:10; 115:2). The form of this taunt is revealing because it is based on what is of central importance for the psalmists. By suggesting that God has forsaken them it acknowledges the fundamental importance to them of God's presence, and by referring to 'your God' or 'their God' it points to the personal nature of God's relationship with his people. Nevertheless it is significant that, although there are many references to mocking or taunting, in no case is it reported that the psalmists responded to the enemies' taunts. Instead they 'held their peace' and refused to speak in their presence, preferring to lay the whole matter before God (38:13; 39:1–2; 62:1–3). Occasionally God is said to address the wicked (50:16–23; 75:4), but the psalmists themselves do not engage in any kind of dialogue with them. Whoever the original enemies may have been, as we saw in Chapter 5 they appear in the psalms as symbolic rather than personal figures. Moreover, the psalmists had no concept of a devil or arch-enemy in personal form (see p. 85). All of this underlines the point that for them evil was something impersonal or subpersonal, which drew people away from God whose nature was essentially personal, and with whom they entered into personal dialogue.

A Dialogue of Persons

This dialogue is between persons. It can take place because both parties share a personal nature, and there is an intimate inner connection between them. This can be illustrated by the fact that the word 'spirit' (*rûaḥ*) is used of both. Human beings have life because the spirit or breath of God is breathed into them (104:30; Gen. 2:7), and they can never escape from the spirit of God (139:7). Although the human spirit is not simply the same as God's spirit, the use of the same word indicates that 'man as *rûaḥ* can only be rightly understood out of God's communication with him.' 'Texts that deal with the *rûaḥ* of God or man show God and man in a dynamic relationship'.[9] The human spirit is that aspect of human beings that is open to the spirit of God, and is capable of a direct person-to-person relationship. Thus the psalmists make it clear that their inner being, their secret inner self and their deepest feelings, are open to and known by God.

> O Lord, all my longing is known to you;
>> my sighing is not hidden from you. (38:9)

> O LORD, you have searched me and known me.
> You know when I sit down and when I rise up;
>> you discern my thoughts from far away. (139:1–2)

Indeed, God knows them better than they know themselves:

> Even before a word is on my tongue,
>> O LORD, you know it completely.
> Such knowledge is too wonderful for me;
>> it is so high that I cannot attain it. (139:4, 6)

This implies that God, who is infinitely greater than we are in his majesty, transcendence and otherness, is nevertheless closer to us than any human person can be. The 'I-You' relation between a person and God is more intimate than that between any two humans. God is present for us in that part of ourselves that is not open to any other human being, the secret, inaccessible place of our own subjectivity and self-consciousness.

We can put this another way by saying that human beings can enter an 'I-You' relationship with God because they too are persons. In modern parlance, a person is an individual self who relates to other persons as a self-conscious 'I'. Indeed, it is widely recognised that we become persons through our relationship with other persons.[10] Through other people we grow into being persons. But at a deeper level, we can recognise that all personhood is derived from God. Just as our life is given us through the medium of human parents but is nevertheless the gift of God, so although our personal nature is given us through our interaction with other human persons, it is ultimately the gift of God. God is the original and basic 'person' from whom all personhood is derived. Our personal nature derives from and is dependent on the personal nature of God. In over-simple language, we exist as persons because God is a 'person'. As self-conscious responsible beings we are able to enter an 'I-You' relationship with God the source of all personhood. Expressed in this way, such a thought may seem far from the language of the Psalms. Nevertheless the psalmists were aware of their dependence on the personal God for their personal being, and they had their own way of expressing it. In more than one place we find the thought that it was the action of God which brought them into being as individual persons.

> Upon you I have leaned from my birth;
> > it was you who took me from my mother's womb. (71:6)
> For it was you who formed my inward parts;
> > you knit me together in my mother's womb.
> I praise you, for I am fearfully and wonderfully made.
> > Wonderful are your works;
> that I know very well.
> > My frame was not hidden from you,
> when I was being made in secret,
> > intricately woven in the depths of the earth. (139:13–15)

These words are a poetic description of a human being's physical origin and development. But we should remember that the biblical writers made no firm distinction between the bodily and mental or spiritual aspects of a person. These verses can, therefore, be read as an account of the formation of a human person as a whole. In the view of the psalmists, it is through the knowledge and activity of God that someone is formed as a human being and becomes a person.

The 'I' of the Psalms

Human personal nature not only derives from the personal nature of God; it is through the 'I-You' relationship with God that it is confirmed and developed. In this relationship a human being is confirmed as an 'I', and knows himself or herself to be a person. The awareness of a greater Other who confronts us in a deep secret part of ourselves that is closed to other people, brings about a unique sense of oneself as a person. One's personal nature is confirmed by a reciprocal relationship with a personal reality who is both over against us and yet united with us in the deepest part of ourselves. Conversely, the absence or withdrawal of this relationship can lead to a profound sense of bottomlessness, of terrifying uncertainty about our very existence as human persons. We find this is expressed in Ps. 22. Here the psalmist feels himself to be abandoned by God, the personal relationship broken. He cries out in despair, repeating the words of intimate relationship: 'My God, my God, why have you forsaken me?' (v. 1). Then he goes on to express the effect of this breakdown on his own sense of who he is: 'I am a worm and not human', (v. 6), or more literally 'no man', the Hebrew word (*'îš*) referring not to humans in general but to individual human beings.[11] Without an 'I-You' relationship with God his sense of himself as a person is undermined. He has 'lost every semblance of humanness'.[12] In these circumstances his only consolation is to remind himself that it was God who brought into being his individual existence:

> Yet it was you who took me from the womb;
>> you kept me safe on my mother's breast.
> On you I was cast from my birth,
>> and since my mother bore me you have been my God. (22:9–10)

It was through an 'I-You' relationship with this personal God that this psalmist both knew himself to be a person, and was confirmed in his personal identity. The same can be said of other Old Testament figures. Writing of the prophets Paul Ricoeur says, 'There is henceforth an "I" because there is a "thou" to whom the prophet addresses himself in the name of God.'[13]

The 'I' of the Psalms is, then, a personal being because of the existence of a personal God, who brought the psalmist into being and to whom the psalmist can relate as a 'You'. It is important to recognise that this is the essential characteristic of this 'I'. There have been many attempts to discover who the original 'I' may have been. Some have argued that the 'I' of the Psalms was the king, and others that he was a cultic official or minister, while others held he was a private individual. But these attempts, while they may be of historical interest, and may shed light on some parts of the Psalter, all fail to grasp the fundamental point. The significance of the 'I' of the Psalms is not that it stands for or represents some particular individual who originally recited the words of the psalms, but that it is constituted by being in the presence of and in dialogue with the personal God. Who the original 'I' may have been – whether the king or anyone else – is of little importance compared with the recognition that the 'I' represents the individual human person, whoever it may be, in relationship with this personal God. The 'I' is, in Mowinckel's words, 'Everyman, i.e. any individual high or low',[14] but it is this individual in an 'I-You' dialogue with God, a partner in an intimate relationship of unity with one who is wholly other, of indivisible closeness with one who remains infinitely transcendent. It is this that provides the basic definition of the 'I' of the Psalter. And it is largely because of this that the Psalms have been the spiritual resource which they have been to so many people of different kinds throughout the centuries.

Deliverance through Being-in-God

For the psalmists it is this relationship with God the personal Other that provides deliverance from evil. We have seen that in the Psalms such deliverance comes about through God's presence, but this happens because this is a personal presence, which draws people into a unique kind of relationship centred in the inmost secret depths of the self, a relationship of being-in-God. It is this that enables the individual truly to *be*, to be a real person linked with the source of all personhood. This relationship with God is thus the most important and fundamental thing in life, the thing to be desired and longed for above all else. There is nothing better in all the world than this relationship (73:25), and the bond of steadfast love (*ḥesed*) which holds it together is better than life itself (63:3). It is this that constitutes deliverance. The 'I-You' relationship preserves a person in life, and saves the individual from nothingness, destruction and death. Since for the psalmists evil is separation from God, the personal bond brought about through God's presence provides deliverance from evil.

This thought is expressed in various ways in a number of psalms.

> To you, O LORD, I call;
>> my rock, do not refuse to hear me,
> for if you are silent to me,
>> I shall be like those who go down to the Pit. (28:1)

Here the psalmist pleads with God to remain in relationship and in dialogue with him, not to refuse to listen or to speak, because a breaking off of this personal relationship would banish him to nothingness, to the place of death. Other psalmists refer to God being 'with us' (23:4; 46:7, 11; 73:23). We can now recognise that this refers not simply to the presence of God, as we saw in the previous chapter, but to a relationship of personal closeness; and it is this that provides security from evil and death (23:4) and from the hostile forces of primordial chaos (46:7, 11). It is the absolute necessity of this bond with God that supplies the most powerful metaphor of longing and need in the psalms, that of thirst:

> As a deer longs for flowing streams,
>> so my soul longs for you, O God.
> My soul thirsts for God,
>> for the living God. (42:1)

Without this relationship life is like a barren and empty land, where a person longs for water and is in danger of fainting without it:

O God, you are my God, I seek you,
   my soul thirsts for you;
my flesh faints for you,
   as in a dry and weary land where there is no water. (63:1)

The longing to be in relationship with God is not just a wish or desire; it is an existential need. Without it personal life is in danger. Cut off from this relationship with God, the 'I' loses personhood, sinks into God-forsaken emptiness and goes down to the Pit. It is this being-in-God alone which delivers from nothingness and evil.

The Individual and the Community

To talk of an 'I-You' relationship in this way may, however, seem excessively individualistic. Evil afflicts not only the individual but the community; it threatens human life as a whole. Deliverance from evil is necessary not just for the one but for the many. Here it is important to notice how the pronoun 'I' is used in the Psalms. Of the 104 psalms which are, in whole or in part, addressed directly to God, a total of 75 are written in the first person singular, in the name of 'I', in at least a part of the psalm. Of these there are some which appear to be straightforwardly prayers of the individual, using 'I' throughout and appearing to speak only in the name of one person. But by far the larger number seem to have been written from a broader perspective, not in the name of the individual only but of a wider community as well. Occasionally both 'I' and 'we' (or 'us') occur within a psalm: see, for example 66:10–13; 75:1, 9; 106:4, 47; 108:1, 13. Often even in psalms which are apparently written entirely in the first person singular it is made clear in a number of ways that others are included as well. Sometimes there is a reference to 'Israel', making it clear that in his personal prayer the psalmist is thinking not only of himself but of the whole people of God. For example, Ps. 22, a very personal lament, turns from saying 'From the horns of the wild oxen you have rescued me' (v. 21), to a call to all Israel to join him in praise:

You who fear the LORD, praise him!
   All you offspring of Jacob, glorify him;
   stand in awe of him, all you offspring of Israel! (v. 23)

We find something similar in 25:22; 130:7–8; 131:3, and in 51:18; 102:13 ('Zion'), all individual laments. Other psalms bring in references to the 'congregation' or the 'great congregation', the assembly of the people, (22:22, 25; 26:12; 35:18; 40:9, 10; 111:1), or more simply to the 'people' (3:8; 28:9; 62:8; 94:14; 116:14; 144:15). Many other individual psalms make it clear that the psalmist has others in mind as well as himself. Sometimes after speaking in his own name the psalmist makes a general statement to show that what is true for him is true for others also:

> And those who know your name put their trust in you,
>> for you, O LORD, have not forsaken those who seek you. (9:10)

> For the LORD is righteous;
> he loves righteous deeds;
>> the upright shall behold his face. (11:7)

> For the LORD hears the needy,
>> and does not despise his own that are in bonds. (69:33)

> I know that the LORD maintains the cause of the needy,
>> and executes justice for the poor. (140:12)

Or in telling of their deliverance the psalmists may call on others to join them in praise:

> Love the LORD, all you his saints.
>> The LORD preserves the faithful. (31:23)

> Be glad in the LORD and rejoice, O righteous,
>> and shout for joy, all you upright in heart. (32:11)

> Sing praises to the LORD, O you his faithful ones,
>> and give thanks to his holy name. (30:4)

A careful reading shows that in all but a few cases, although the 'psalms of the individual' were written out of the experience of individual people, they had a wider group of people in mind as well. Indeed, it becomes doubtful whether a clear line can be drawn between 'individual' and 'community' psalms, as is commonly done.[15]

The notion that the 'I' of the Psalter includes and represents more than the individual is, of course, not a new one. It has appeared in psalm studies in two slightly different ways in past decades. On the one hand some have held, as we have seen, that in many individual psalms the 'I' was the king, speaking and acting in a representative capacity on behalf of all the people.[16] On the other hand some scholars of an earlier period maintained that the ancient Israelites did not have a developed sense of the individual, and that a social unit or 'kin-group' was viewed as a 'corporate personality', and could be spoken of as if it were an individual. Seen in either of these ways the 'I' of the Psalms can be understood, not as a single individual in the modern sense, but as a way of representing a larger social group, the nation or the family.[17]

There may be truth in this, provided that it is not taken to mean that the community was the primary thing, that the 'I' was only a representation of the wider group, and that the individual had no independent standing. Such a view would conflict with the character of many of the individual psalms. It is hard to believe that the expression of heartfelt emotion, and the description of the experience of distress or of joy, represent the feelings of a 'corporate personality' or formal sentiments of the king spoken on behalf of the people. Rather than assume that the individual was subsumed in the corporate, it is better to view the experience of the individual as the basic thing on which the life of the wider group depends. A reading of the Old Testament as a whole suggests that in the view of the biblical writers God's dealings with his people took place primarily through individuals. The people of Israel came into being through God's call to one man, Abraham:

> He was but one when I called him,
> but I blessed him and made him many. (Isa. 51:2)

And it was the experience of the individual person which formed the basis of the people's subsequent experience of God. Whatever may be the literal historical truth of the stories of Abraham, Isaac, and Jacob, of Moses, Samuel, David, and Solomon, or of the call of the prophets Isaiah, Jeremiah, Hosea and Amos, they point strongly to the belief that God worked through individuals and their personal experience for the sake of all. Sometimes it is emphasised that God did significant work for his people through individuals when they were 'alone' or 'in isolation' (*lᵉbaddô* or *bādād*): Jacob (Gen. 32:24); Moses (Exod. 24:2); Jeremiah (Jer. 15:17). For Israel the experience of the individual was paradigmatic, and the religious life of the nation was to a considerable degree both formed by it and seen in terms of it. But God's work with the individual was never done for the sake of that person alone, but for the community as a whole. The 'I' of the Psalms, therefore, is not an isolated individual. Throughout the Psalter the individual and the people are linked together. There is no 'I' without a 'we', but the 'I' is primary. It is the basis of all

God's dealings with his people. It has been widely held that in Israelite thought the individual partakes of the salvation of the community;[19] but probably it was the other way around. It could be said that the people were incorporated into the individual, rather than vice versa – a way of thinking that provides the pattern for the later Christian doctrine that members of the church are incorporated into Christ. Through being incorporated into the 'I' – the individual who was a person before God – the community became a 'community of persons' before God. The one contained the many, and the people's knowledge and experience of God took place through the experience of the individual.

To focus on the individual's personal relationship with a personal God in the Psalms, therefore, is not to retreat into individualism; it is to recognise that this 'I-You' relationship is the basis and pattern of the community's relationship with God. When the psalmists speak of the individual's experience of evil and deliverance they are speaking also of the community, because in this experience the whole community was involved. In the individual's experience of enemies the whole community experienced the lurking, insidious power of evil. In the individual's experience of the deep waters the whole community felt the danger of being submerged and overwhelmed by the chaotic floods of chaos and death. In the sense of God-forsakenness felt by the individual the whole community experienced the sense of being separated from God and cut off from the source of life. And it was through the individual's awareness of the presence of God and entry into a person-to-person 'I-You' relationship with God, that the community could share in this relationship with the personal God, and in the deliverance and protection from evil which this relationship provided. For the community deliverance from evil would come about through the emergence of a community of persons in true personal relationship with one another as well as with God.

Seen in this way, the Psalms offer us a way of understanding evil and deliverance from it, both for the individual and the community. In them the psalmists addressed God directly or indirectly, in the name of 'I' or of 'we' or of the community more generally. In their prayer-poems they used a rich variety of images to express their sense of the threat imposed by hostile evil forces which surrounded them and sought to separate them from God; and to express their trust in and their yearning for the God in whose presence evil cannot stand, and in whose personal keeping there is deliverance and protection. In addressing God in this way they not only brought themselves into God's presence, but also engaged with God in a relationship in which both individuals and members of the community could find their true selves as persons, and know themselves to be held and bound and kept by God. It was for this that they longed and thirsted because it alone provided deliverance and protection from the forces of evil.

Notes

Chapter 1: Poems and Prayers

1. See the introduction to Briggs' commentary, p.xxi. The word *t*pillôt ('prayers') is used in Ps. 72:20 with reference to some of the psalms.
2. Recent studies of Hebrew poetry include: Kugel, *The Idea of Biblical Poetry*; Alter, *The Art of Biblical Poetry*; Watson, *Classical Hebrew Poetry*; Gillingham, *The Poems and Psalms of the Hebrew Bible*; Schökel, *A Manual of Hebrew Poetics*; and two essays by Miller, 'The Theological Significance of Biblical Poetry', and 'Meter, Parallelism and Tropes' in *Israelite Religion and Biblical Theology*. A useful summary is found in Magonet, *A Rabbi Reads the Psalms*, Chapter 2: 'Biblical Poetry for Beginners'.
3. Terrien, *The Elusive Presence*, p. 337.
4. Miller, *Interpreting the Psalms*, p. 17.
5. Lewis, *The Poetic Image*, pp. 26ff.
6. See Brock, *The Luminous Eye*, pp. 23ff.
7. Kraus, *Theology of the Psalms*, p. 15, quoting Hegel.
8. See for example, Watson, *Classical Hebrew Poetry*, pp. 97ff for a discussion of metrical forms based on the number of stresses in a line.
9. Kugel, in *The Idea of Biblical Poetry*, argues that it is a mistake to look for metre in Hebrew poetry. Schökel places emphasis on the sounds of Hebrew poetry, and prefers to speak of 'rhythm' rather than metre, *A Manual of Hebrew Poetics*, pp. 20ff and 34ff.
10. See especially Kugel, *ibid.*, Chapter 1. Kugel concludes that parallelism takes many forms, its main characteristic being that the second half of the verse line 'seconds' the first, 'carrying it further, echoing it, defining it, restating it, contrasting with it', p. 51.
11. Miller, 'The Theological Significance of Biblical Poetry', in *Israelite Religion and Biblical Theology*, pp. 235ff.
12. See Kugel, *The Idea of Biblical Poetry*, pp. 76ff.
13. Alter believes that Kugel 'comes perilously close to concluding that there is no poetry in the Bible, only a "continuum" from loosely parallelistic structures in what we think of as the prose sections, to a more "heightened rhetoric" of parallelistic devices in what we misleadingly label verse'; Alter, *The Art of Biblical Poetry*, p. 4.
14. On the importance of ambiguity for poetry see Miller, 'The Theological Significance of Biblical Poetry', in *Israelite Religion and Biblical Theology*, pp. 245ff.
15. A phrase used frequently by Kugel in *The Idea of Biblical Poetry*; see p. 71 and passim.
16. A device referred to technically as '*qtl-yqtl* alternation'.
17. Miller, 'Meter, Parallelism and Tropes' in *Israelite Religion and Biblical Theology*, p. 256. He adds (p. 257) that 'the figurative language of biblical poetry should be – and of course is – able to tell us much about Israel's experience and how they assimilated and understood it.' It is this belief that underlies this book.
18. Of the 150 psalms, 104 are addressed, in whole or at least in some small part, to God; a further 27 include a summons to worship or praise God, or to approach him in some way; almost all the remaining 19 appear to refer in some way to the establishment of a relationship with God.
19. B. W. Anderson, *Out of the Depths*, p. ix.
20. See Uriel Simon, *Four Approaches to the Book of Psalms*, especially Chapter 1.

Chapter 2: Interpreting the Psalms

1. For the Canaanite background to Ps. 29 see Cross, *Canaanite Myth and Hebrew Epic*, pp. 150ff; Day, *Yahweh and the Gods and Goddesses of Canaan*, pp. 99ff. On Ps. 19 see Day *ibid.*, p. 162. This view of Pss 29 and 19 is taken by most commentators, see e.g. Kraus and A. A. Anderson.
2. Grant and Tracy, *A Short History of the Interpretation of the Bible*, p. 21.
3. English translation in Braude, *The Midrash on Psalms*.
4. Delitzsch, *Biblical Commentary of the Psalms*, p. 73.
5. Levine, *Sing unto God a New Song*, pp. 6f.
6. *ibid.*, p. 4.
7. R. Loewe, 'Jewish Exegesis', in Coggins and Houlden (eds), *Dictionary of Biblical Interpretation*, p. 349.
8. Braude, *The Midrash on Psalms*, p. xx.
9. *ibid.*, 1.4, p. 7. The psalms are quoted here as they are given in Braude.
10. *ibid.*, 22.19, pp. 315f.
11. The foregoing quotations are all from Young, *The Art of Performance*, pp. 90f.
12. Augustine, *Expositions on the Book of Psalms*, Vol. I, pp. 1f.
13. *ibid.*, Vol. I, pp. 168f.
14. Grant and Tracy, *A Short History of the Interpretation of the Bible*, pp. 73ff.
15. G. R. Evans, 'Mediaeval Interpretation', in Coggins and Houlden (eds) *Dictionary of Biblical Interpretation*, p. 439.
16. Delitzsch, *Biblical Commentary of the Psalms*, p. 74.
17. 'Rarely were they [the early rabbis] interested in a whole psalm, unless it allowed them to teach an interesting lesson', Levine, *Sing unto God a New Song*, p. 4.
18. Saadiah believed that the Psalms were all written by David and were commandments from God. Others maintained that they were human 'prophetic prayers' which pointed forward to future events such as the exile, or to the messiah. Some even proposed a late, post-exilic date for some of the Psalms. A full discussion of these different views is found in Uriel Simon, *Four Approaches to the Book of Psalms*.
19. R. Loewe, 'Jewish Exegesis', in Coggins and Houlden (eds) *Dictionary of Biblical Interpretation*, p. 350.
20. Levine, *Sing unto God a New Song*, p. 10.
21. *Tehillim*, p. 92.
22. Levine, *Sing unto God a New Song*, p. 13.
23. Luther, *Works, Vol. 14: Selected Psalms III*, pp. 191, 194.
24. Buttenwieser, *The Psalms*, p. 587.
25. Westermann, *Praise and Lament in the Psalms*. Westermann's work has been taken further by Broyles, *The Conflict of Faith and Experience in the Psalms*.
26. Mowinckel, *The Psalms in Israel's Worship*.
27. Birkeland, *The Evildoers in the Book of Psalms*; Johnson, *The Cultic Prophet and Israel's Psalmody*; Eaton, *Kingship and the Psalms*; Croft, *The Identity of the Individual in the Psalms*.
28. A fuller discussion of the limitations of the historical-critical approach is found in Nasuti, *Defining the Sacred Songs*, pp. 49ff.
29. The lack of consensus on the date of the Psalms can be illustrated by the fact that, after decades of debate we find one scholar writing in 1948 that 'The great majority of psalms was presumably written . . . between 400 and 100 BC and shortly before, in the fifth century', (Pfeiffer, *Introduction to the Old Testament*, p. 629); and another, writing in 1949, that 'the majority of the psalms came into existence in the pre-exilic period of Israel's history' (that is, no later than the 7th century BC), Weiser, *The Psalms*, p. 91.
30. See Levine, *Sing unto God a New Song*, pp. 18f.
31. e.g. Eaton, *Kingship and the Psalms*, pp. 36ff.

32. The fact that we have no difficulty in accepting conflicting metaphors as part of poetry can be illustrated by referring to a well-known hymn of Charles Wesley: 'Jesu, Lover of my soul,/ Let me to thy bosom fly,/ While the nearer waters roll,/ While the tempest still is high/ . . . Safe into the haven guide.' If this were a biblical psalm, some scholars might well be troubled at the mixing of the metaphors of bosom and haven, and some might wonder whether Wesley was in a storm at sea when he wrote the poem!

33. Nasuti, *Defining the Sacred Songs*, pp. 19f.

34. For a balanced discussion of recent approaches see Barton, *Reading the Old Testament*.

35. For an interpretation of the Psalms as prayer poems see Schaefer's commentary in the Berit Olam series, and especially his Introduction.

36. The view that some aspects of a historical-critical approach can usefully be held along with more recent 'post-modern' interpretative methods is elaborated in Barton, *Reading the Old Testament*; Barr, *The Concept of Biblical Theology*; Brown, *Tradition and Imagination*.

Chapter 3: Poetic Imagery

1. S. J. Brown, *Image and Truth*, p. 19.

2. Caird, *Language and Imagery of the Bible*, p. 152.

3. Lewis, *The Poetic Image*, p. 18.

4. *ibid.*, p. 40.

5. *ibid.*, p. 28.

6. Quoted in Lewis, *ibid.*, p. 141.

7. *ibid.*, p. 142.

8. Jacobi, *Complex, Archetype, Symbol in the Psychology of C. G. Jung*, p. 31.

9. Samuels *et al.*, *A Critical Dictionary of Jungian Analysis*, p. 27.

10. Lewis, *The Poetic Image*, p. 143.

11. Caird, *Language and Imagery of the Bible*, p. 152.

12. Alter, *The Art of Biblical Poetry*, p. 112.

13. *ibid.*, p. 113.

14. Lewis, *The Poetic Image*, p. 45.

15. Alter, *The Art of Biblical Poetry*, p. 189.

16. See Johnson, *The Cultic Prophet in Israel's Psalmody*.

17. See Tournay, *Seeing and Hearing in the Psalms*.

18. Kraus, *Theology of the Psalms*, p. 139.

19. Miller, *Interpreting the Psalms*, p. 52.

20. Jacobi, *Complex, Archetype, Symbol in the Psychology of C. G. Jung*, p. 99.

21. *ibid.*

22. See the discussion in Rogerson, *Myth in Old Testament Interpretation*, and Childs, *Myth and Reality in the Old Testament*.

23. Rogerson, *Myth in Old Testament Interpretation*, p. 175.

24. Hooke (ed.), *Myth and Ritual*, p. 3.

25. Childs, *Myth and Reality in the Old Testament*, p. 30.

26. von Rad, *Old Testament Theology*, Vol. II, p. 81.

27. *ibid.*, p. 349.

28. Birkeland, *The Evildoers in the Book of Psalms*, p. 31.

29. See especially Cross, *Canaanite Myth and Hebrew Epic*, and Day, *Yahweh and the Gods and Goddesses of Canaan*.

30. Cross, *Canaanite Myth and Hebrew Epic*, p. 143.

31. See the discussion in Levenson, *Creation and the Persistence of Evil*; Murray, *The Cosmic Covenant*; and Cross, *Canaanite Myth and Hebrew Epic*.

32. Mowinckel, *The Psalms in Israel's Worship*, Vol. I, p. 244.

33. Caird, *Language and Imagery of the Bible*, p. 232.

34. Wakeman, *God's Battle with the Monster*, p. 105.
35. Kraus, *Theology of the Psalms*, p. 134.
36. Caird, *Language and Imagery of the Bible*, p. 232.

Chapter 4: Evil and Distress

1. For example, both von Rad in his *Old Testament Theology* and A. A. Anderson in his commentary on the Psalms discuss the theological meaning of many Hebrew words in some detail, including the various words for 'sin', but in neither case does the word *ra'* appear in the index of Hebrew words discussed. Eichrodt deals with some questions to do with 'evil' but without any discussion of the meaning of the Hebrew words.
2. The two meanings are brought out clearly in the short article on 'Evil' in Richardson, *A Theological Word Book of the Bible*, pp. 73f.
3. Kraus, *Theology of the Psalms*, p. 131.
4. See Keel, *The Symbolism of the Biblical World*, pp. 84f; Mowinckel, *The Psalms in Israel's Worship*, Vol. II, p. 7.
5. Lindström, *Sin and Suffering*, p. 39.
6. Kraus, *Psalms*, Vol. I, p. 148.
7. Quoted in Kraus, *Psalms*, Vol. I, p. 164.
8. Broyles, *The Conflict of Faith and Experience in the Psalms*, p. 189.
9. Radak (Rabbi David Kimshi) quoted in *Tehillim*, p. 426.
10. Keel, *The Symbolism of the Biblical World*, p. 66.
11. A. A.Anderson, *Psalms*, pp. 129, 627.
12. *ibid.*, p. 500.
13. Kraus, *Psalms*, Vol. II, p. 285.
14. *Tehillim*, p. 526.
15. See Broyles, *The Conflict of Faith and Experience in the Psalms*, p. 205.
16. A view taken by Sandford in *Evil: the Shadow Side of Reality*, pp. 26ff. Sandford follows Jung in maintaining that Isa. 45:5–7 and Amos 3:6 show that the Israelites believed that Yhwh was the source of moral evil as well as good.
17. See Broyles, *The Conflict of Faith and Experience in the Psalms*, p. 219.
18. A theme developed at length in Brueggeman, *Theology of the Old Testament*, see especially pp. 321ff.

Chapter 5: Images of Distress: (1) Hostility

1. A useful summary of the issues is found in Kraus, *Psalms*, Vol. I, pp. 95ff.
2. Most strikingly, Birkeland in *The Evildoers in the Book of Psalms* maintains unequivocally that '[t]he enemies are the [foreign] nations'; 'the evildoers . . . are gentiles in all cases'; 'private enemies do not seem to be mentioned in the Book of Psalms'; pp.17, 93, 46, and passim. In keeping with this view, Birkeland sees the Psalms as narrowly nationalistic, with limited religious content: 'Their *literary* value is . . . mostly greater than that of their religious content, which keeps to the nationalistic core of extreme exclusivity', p. 46.
3. See Kraus, *Psalms* on all the psalms listed here.
4. Kraus, *Theology of the Psalms*, p. 128.
5. See A. A. Anderson, *Psalms*, on Pss 13:4 and 31:8.
6. Lindström, *Suffering and Sin*, p. 83.
7. 'We first find a figure that in some way corresponds to our definition of the devil in the *Book of Watchers*' (4th century BCE), Sacchi, *The History of the Second Temple Period*, p. 344.
8. A. A. Anderson, *Psalms*, p. 102.

9. But the 'wicked' is a broad category, not exclusively identified with the 'enemies'. See Croft, *The Identity of the Individual in the Psalms*, pp. 20ff.
10. Kraus, *Theology of the Psalms*, p. 130.
11. See Botterweck and Ringgren, *Theological Dictionary of the Old Testament*, Vol. I, pp. 140f.
12. Mowinckel, *The Psalms in Israel's Worship*, Vol. II, p. 7.
13. Eaton, *Psalms*, p. 41; see also Lindström, *Suffering and Sin*, pp. 147f.
14. Kraus, *Theology of the Psalms*, p. 28.
15. *ibid.*, p. 29.
16. Ricoeur, *The Symbolism of Evil*, p. 199.
17. Eaton, *Psalms*, p. 92.
18. Lindström, *Suffering and Sin*, p. 440.
19. Keel, *The Symbolism of the Biblical World*, p. 85.
20. Eaton, *Psalms*, p. 163.
21. Eaton, *Kingship and the Psalms*, pp. 35, 140.
22. *Tehillim*, p. 106.
23. Davidson, *The Vitality of Worship*, p. 52.
24. Miller, *Interpreting the Psalms*, p. 50.
25. Lindström, *Suffering and Sin*, p. 84.
26. Kraus, *Psalms*, p. 98.
27. Ricoeur, *The Symbolism of Evil*, p. 196.
28. Davidson, *The Vitality of Worship*, p. 183.
29. Keel, *The Symbolism of the Biblical World*, p. 85.
30. Ps. 68:30 also apparently refers to bulls, but the meaning is not clear and the text may be corrupt. The psalmist appears to have Egypt in mind.
31. *Tehillim*, p. 280.
32. Keel, *The Symbolism of the Biblical World*, p. 86.
33. See Kraus, *Psalms*, p. 297 on Ps. 22:12.
34. Davidson, *The Vitality of Worship*, p. 80.
35. Keel, *The Symbolism of the Biblical World*, p. 87.
36. Eaton, *Psalms*, p. 86.
37. Kraus, *Psalms*, p. 297.
38. Gray, *The Biblical Doctrine of the Reign of God*, p. 96.
39. Davidson, *The Vitality of Worship*, p. 216.
40. Weiser, *Psalms*, p. 223. Weiser doubts whether the wild beasts were thought of as actual demons.
41. Eaton, *Psalms*, p. 73.
42. Keel, *The Symbolism of the Biblical World*, p. 88.
43. *ibid.*, p. 72.
44. *ibid.*, p. 89.
45. Brown, Driver and Briggs, *Hebrew and English Lexicon of the Old Testament*, p. 430.
46. A. A. Anderson, *Psalms*, p. 462.
47. Miller, *Interpreting the Psalms*, p. 25.
48. The Greek word *pagis*, used for a snare in the New Testament and in the saying of St Antony, (see Ward, *The Sayings of the Desert Fathers*, Anthony the Great 7, p. 2) is the word frequently used in the LXX to translate the Hebrew words for snare, or trap. And there is an interesting use of its verbal form in relation to hostility to Jesus in Matt. 22:15 ('. . . plotted to entrap him').

Chapter 6: **Images of Distress: (2) Being Overwhelmed**

1. Albright, *The Archeology of Palestine*, pp. 113, 210.

2. This question is discussed at length in Kirkpatrick, *The Psalms*, pp. 396ff; see also A. A. Anderson, *Psalms*, pp. 500.
3. Davidson, *The Vitality of Worship*, p. 111.
4. Eichrodt, *Theology of the Old Testament*, Vol. II, p. 114n.
5. Day, *God's Conflict with the Dragon and the Sea*, p. 179.
6. The text of the myth is found in Pritchard, (ed.) *Ancient Near Eastern Texts*, pp. 129–144, and summarised in Cross, *Canaanite Myth and Hebrew Epic*, pp. 112ff.
7. See Pritchard, (ed.) *Ancient Near Eastern Texts*, p.131.
8. See Cross, *Canaanite Myth and Hebrew Epic*, p. 119.
9. Day, *God's Conflict with the Dragon and the Sea*, p. 179; Wakeman, *God's Battle with the Monster*, p. 79.
10. Wakeman, *God's Battle with the Monster*, pp. 79, 102.
11. A. A. Anderson, *Psalms*, p. 621.
12. Day, *God's Conflict with the Dragon and the Sea*, p. 188.
13. Day, *Psalms*, p. 82.
14. Levenson, *Creation and the Persistence of Evil*, pp. 15, 17, 18.
15. *Tehillim*, p. 1104.
16. Davidson, *The Vitality of Worship*, p. 310.
17. May, 'Some Cosmic Connotations of *Mayim Rabbîm*', p. 11.
18. Gray, *The Biblical Doctrine of the Reign of God*, p. 43.
19. Gibson, *Language and Imagery in the Old Testament*, p. 102.
20. Brown, *Discipleship and Imagination*, p. 167.
21. Brueggemann, *Theology of the Old Testament*, pp. 534ff; May, 'Some Cosmic Connotations of *Mayim Rabbîm*', p. 11. Such a dualism is also clearly implied in Levenson, *Creation and the Persistence of Evil*.
22. Levenson, *Creation and the Persistence of Evil*, p. 19.
23. Wakeman, *God's Battle with the Monster*, p. 88.
24. The variety of uses of the image of the pit is set out in Ryken *et al., Dictionary of Biblical Imagery*.
25. Kraus, *Psalms*, Vol. I, p. 162, quoting Köhler and von Rad.
26. Braude, *The Midrash on Psalms*, p. 432 on Ps. 40:2; *Tehillim*, p. 361, on Ps. 30:3.
27. Davidson, *The Vitality of Worship*, p. 66.
28. Wakeman, *God's Battle with the Monster*, p. 106.
29. Keel, *The Symbolism of the Biblical World*, p. 64.
30. Lindström, *Sin and Suffering*, p. 207.
31. Brueggemann, *Theology of the Old Testament*, p. 554.
32. Lindström, *Sin and Suffering*, p. 209.
33. Kraus, *Psalms*, Vol. II, pp. 183, 193.

Chapter 7: Images of Distress: (3) Separation from God

1. Caird, *The Language and Imagery of the Bible*, p. 152.
2. Kraus, *Psalms*, Vol. II, p. 9.
3. Eaton, *Psalms*, p. 157.
4. See especially Gouldner, *The Psalms of the Sons of Korah*, p. 24ff.
5. Lindström, *Sin and Suffering*, p. 80.
6. *ibid.*, p. 49.
7. Eaton, *Psalms*, p. 104.
8. Kraus, *Psalms*, Vol. II, p. 157.
9. Eaton, *Psalms*, p. 57.
10. Davidson, *The Vitality of Worship*, p. 58.
11. This point is demonstrated in Balentine, *The Hidden God*, p. 166; see also Ryrie, *Silent Waiting*, pp. 113ff.

12. A. A. Anderson, *Psalms*, p. 243.

Chapter 8: Evil in the Psalms: A Summary

1. Ricoeur, *The Symbolism of Evil*, p. 258.
2. von Rad, *Old Testament Theology*, Vol. I, p. 152.
3. Levenson, *Creation and the Persistence of Evil*, p. xxi.
4. Brueggemann, *Theology of the Old Testament*, p. 158.
5. Kraus, *Theology of the Psalms*, p. 63.
6. See Chapter 6, note 21.
7. Eichrodt, *Theology of the Old Testament*, Vol. II, p. 405.
8. Lindström, *Sin and Suffering*, p. 11.
9. See Chapter 5, note 7.
10. Mowinckel, *The Psalms in Israel's Worship*, Vol. I, p. 108.
11. Wakeman, *God's Battle with the Monster*, p. 126.
12. Levenson, *Creation and the Persistence of Evil*, p. xxiii.
13. Caird, *The Language and Imagery of the Bible*, p. 242.
14. von Rad, *Old Testament Theology*, Vol. I, p. 144.
15. Davidson, *The Vitality of Worship*, p. 272.
16. Mowinckel, *The Psalms in Israel's Worship*, Vol. I, p. 152.
17. Kraus, *Psalms*, passim.
18. Brueggemann, *Theology of the Old Testament*, pp. 534ff.
19. Quoted in Kraus, *Psalms*, Vol. I, p. 214, n.1.
20. Kraus, *Theology of the Psalms*, p. 135, quoting Gunkel and Begrich.
21. Ricoeur, *The Symbolism of Evil*, pp. 87f.
22. The Hebrew Bible has no clear word for 'punish'. The verbs *y-k-ḥ*, to 'adjudge' or 'reprove', *y-s-r*, 'to chastise', and *p-q-d*, 'to visit' are all sometimes translated 'punish'. But there is a strong idea that punishment is bound up with the misdeed, that the guilt is itself the punishment, with the result that the word *'āwōn*, 'guilt', can often be used in the sense of punishment, as in 69:27; ('punishment', RSV; 'guilt', NRSV).
23. Augustine, *Expositions on the Book of Psalms*, Vol. I, p. 30.
24. Eichrodt, *Theology of the Old Testament*, Vol. II, p. 404.
25. In the light of this it is worth considering whether there is an over-emphasis on sin and sins, as opposed to evil, in Christian preaching and liturgy.
26. Ricoeur, *The Symbolism of Evil*, pp. 313f.
27. *ibid.*, p. 156.
28. Levenson, *Creation and the Persistence of Evil*, p. 49.

Chapter 9: Images of Deliverance: (1) God the Protector

1. Much the most common are the verbs *n-ṣ-l* (hiphil), usually translated 'to deliver' (42 times in the Psalter), and *y-š-'* (hiphil), usually translated 'to save' (44 times). Other words are found less frequently.
2. Johnson, *The Cultic Prophet and Israel's Psalmody*, p. 330.
3. A. A. Anderson, *Psalms*, p. 72.
4. In 84:9 some versions (e.g. KJV following LXX) take 'shield' to be in apposition to 'God' and translate 'O God our shield'. Jewish commentators recognised that it could be 'a prayer for the king' or 'a reference to God himself', *Tehillim*, p. 1057. Similarly, 89:18 may be translated 'The Lord is our shield'.
5. Eaton, *Psalms*, p. 209; see also p. 88 on 28:7.
6. Kraus, *Psalms*, Vol. I, p. 158.
7. *Tehillim*, p. 99.
8. *ibid.*, p. 422.
9. A. A. Anderson, *Psalms*, p. 836; Davidson, *The Vitality of Worship*, p. 20.

10. A. A. Anderson, *Psalms*, p. 788; Weiser, *The Psalms*, p. 717.
11. *Tehillim*, p. 369.
12. A. A. Anderson, *Psalms*, p. 315.
13. *ibid.*, p. 334.
14. The rock represents 'the security of solid ground rather than its rigid unyielding closedness', Wakeman, *God's Battle with the Monster*, p. 138.
15. Keel, *The Symbolism of the Biblical World*, p. 72.
16. Kraus, *Psalms*, Vol. I, p. 259.
17. *ibid.*, Vol. II, p. 9.
18. A. A. Anderson, *Psalms*, pp. 447f.
19. There is another view, that behind the metaphor of the wings 'is the symbol of the winged disc of the sun, so well known in Egypt and Mesopotamia'; but, as Anderson says, this seems unlikely. A. A. Anderson, *Psalms*, p. 289.
20. Lam. 4:20. See also Kraus, *Psalms*, Vol. I. p. 248.
21. 'The sanctuary . . . is indicated by means of the image of the outstretched wings of the cherubim,' Kraus, *Psalms*, Vol. I, p. 399.
22. Ps. 17:8 has literally, 'Guard me as the apple of the daughter of the eye' (*kᵉ'îšôn bath-'āyin*), whereas Deut. 32:10 has 'guarding him as the apple of his eye' (*kᵉ'îšôn 'ênô*) and Prov. 7:2 has 'Keep my teaching as the apple of your eye' (*kᵉ'îšôn 'êneykā*).
23. Kirkpatrick, *Psalms*, p. 81.
24. Kraus, *Theology of the Psalms*, p. 160.
25. Kraus, *Psalms*, Vol. II, p. 532, and Vol. I, p. 241.

Chapter 10: Images of Deliverance: (2) Under God's Protection

1. *Tehillim*, p. 83.
2. A. A. Anderson, *Psalms*, p. 160.
3. The Hebrew text (MT) does not make satisfactory sense, but the translation suggested here probably gives the intended meaning. Cf A. A. Anderson, *Psalms*, p. 212: '[T]rouble is seen as a condition of being hemmed in, while deliverance consists of "giving freedom" by bringing the oppressed into a broad place.'
4. Although Barr (*The Semantics of Biblical Language*) has shown that this is broadly true, the use of *sar*, meaning 'narrowness' or 'restriction' to indicate trouble or distress, gives reason to think that being saved from distress may be thought of as coming into a wide or broad space.
5. 'The Hebrew *y-š-'* ['to save'] is usually linked with the Arabic *waśi'a* ("to be wide, broad"), and thus its basic meaning may be "to be wide", and in a causative form it would suggest "to give room", hence "to deliver"', A. A. Anderson, *Psalms*, p. 409. See also Kraus, *Psalms*, Vol. I, pp. 139, 248.
6. Kraus, *Psalms*, Vol. I, p. 148.
7. Kirkpatrick, *The Psalms*, p. 97.
8. *Tehillim*, p. 371.
9. The word translated 'level' is related to the word usually translated 'upright', and so this verse is sometimes regarded as a prayer to be led 'on the path of integrity' (*Tehillim*, p. 335) or 'in what is right' (Weiser, *The Psalms*, p. 253); but this removes the power of the image.
10. The NRSV 'level path' in 143:10 follows the BHS margin; the MT reads 'level ground'.
11. Kirkpatrick, *The Psalms*, p. 143.
12. Oesterley, *The Psalms*, p. 197.
13. Lindström, *Sin and Suffering*, pp. 160f.
14. Anderson, *Psalms*, p. 252.
15. Kraus, *Psalms*, Vol. I, p. 364.

16. The familiar words 'the shadow of death' are given in the NRSV margin (and in the RSV). The NRSV text reads 'the darkest valley'. Either translation is possible.

17. 'Drawing near to God . . . indicates the experience of God mediated through the Temple', Eaton, *Psalms*, p. 186.

18. '[T]he nearness of God means deliverance and protection', A. A. Anderson, *Psalms*, p. 843, on 119:151.

19. Kraus, *Psalms*, Vol. I, p. 386.

20. It is generally believed that Ps. 46 represents a tradition which regarded the temple itself as a source of security; but the psalm makes it clear that the city is secure only in so far as 'God is in the midst of her'.

21. The Hebrew phrase translated 'very present' means literally 'very much found', and the clause can be read to mean 'he has fully proved himself to be a reliable help', (A. A. Anderson, *Psalms*, p. 355). But the phrase can be used generally for being present or available, 2 Chr. 15:2; Jer. 29:14 (see Kirkpatrick, *Psalms*, p. 255). The Midrash paraphrases: 'He is near to us at every trouble that comes upon us' (Braude, *The Midrash on Psalms*, p. 456).

22. The Hebrew verb *l-q-h*, to take or receive, is used of both the Old Testament figures who were taken up into heaven without dying; Enoch (Gen. 5:24) and Elijah (2 Kings 2:10). On this issue see especially Davidson, *The Vitality of Worship*, pp. 162, 235f.

23. The NRSV rendering, 'all who sleep', is an emendation of the Hebrew text, but the same meaning is conveyed by the next line. E. Davis in a study of Ps. 22 comments that this 'departs sharply from the much more common view that the insentient dead are incapable of offering praise'. ('Exploding the Limits', p. 143).

24. von Rad comments, 'Yhwh holds his pious one fast, and remains his God in every situation in life, and even death cannot remove the communion vouchsafed to him.' 'The communion with Yhwh is one that cannot be destroyed.' (*Old Testament Theology* Vol. I, pp. 406, 407).

25. Quoted in Weiser, *The Psalms*, p. 515. NRSV translates this verse, 'There is nothing on earth that I desire other than you' (similarly RSV); but this does not bring out the sense that it is '*when I have you*' that I desire nothing else. JPS has, 'Having You I want no one on earth.'

26. The phrase translated 'give me an undivided heart' is literally 'unite my heart' (RSV). This can refer either to unity or integrity of heart ('let me be one in heart' NEB), or to a heart that is united to or in union with God. See A. A. Anderson, *Psalms*, p. 617, Davidson, *The Vitality of Worship*, p. 285.

27. Perhaps it was because the root of the word *bar* ('pure') had associations with 'clear' or even 'shining' (Brown, Driver and Briggs, *A Hebrew and English Lexicon of the Old Testament*, pp. 140f) that the idea of purity of heart came to be connected with clarity of vision, as in Matt. 5:8, 'Blessed are the pure in heart, for they shall see God'. In this way the heart can be said to have eyes: 'with the eyes of your heart enlightened', Eph. 1:18; 'through him the eyes of our hearts were opened', 1 Clement 36. The idea was taken further by the Syriac fathers, especially Ephrem, with their emphasis on the need for a 'luminous' (ie. clear, pure, transparent or limpid) heart, in order to be able to see things with a 'luminous eye', (Brock, *Syriac Fathers*, pp. xxixff; *The Luminous Eye*, p. 39). See also I. Nowell, 'The Concept of Purity of Heart in the Old Testament' in Luckman and Kulzer (eds), *Purity of Heart in Early Ascetic and Monastic Literature*, pp.17–29.

28. Levenson, *Creation and the Persistence of Evil*, p. xvii.

Chapter 11: Addressing God as Person

1. Miller, *Israelite Religion and Biblical Theology*, p. 244.

2. Buber, *I and Thou*, p. 161.

3. *ibid.*, p. 181. Buber adds that God is more properly thought of as the 'absolute person'. He could be said to be 'suprapersonal'.

4. von Rad, *Genesis*, p. 117.

5. In 40 of the 54 instances, the words are addressed directly to God. In 45 the word used for God is *ᵉlōhîm* and in 9 it is *ʼēl*.

6. Eaton in particular regards the phrase 'My God' as a sign that the psalm is royal; *Kingship and the Psalms*, pp. 170ff. However, of the 34 psalms which contain the phrase, only 23 are in Eaton's own list of royal psalms. The fact that the phrase occurs in 11 psalms which he himself does not regard as royal shows that the words were not used exclusively by the king. Croft concludes that while the presence of divine epithets to which the first-person singular suffix is attached can be a mark of royal style, this does not seem to apply to the phrase 'My God'. Croft, *The Identity of the Individual in the Psalms*, p. 79.

7. The fact that exactly the same words, 'Depart (or go away) from me . . .' (*sûrû mimmennî*) are found in 119:115 and 6:8 suggests that it may have been a kind of formula.

8. These include the 'cursing' psalms 58 and 109, and others which use a jussive form inviting God to let something unpleasant or disastrous happen to the enemies, as e.g. in 40:14f; 35:4ff.

9. Wolff, *Anthropology of the Old Testament*, p. 39.

10. See especially Macmurray, *Persons in Relation*. For example in p. 61: 'the unit of personal existence is not the individual but two persons in personal relation . . . We are persons not by individual right but in virtue of our relation to one another. The personal is constituted by personal relatedness.'

11. Hastings, *Dictionary of the Bible*, Vol. III, p. 225.

12. Kraus, *Psalms*, Vol. I, p. 295 on Ps. 22:6.

13. Ricoeur, *The Symbolism of Evil*, p. 103.

14. Mowinckel, *the Psalms in Israel's Worship*, Vol. II, p. 1.

15. See e.g. B. W. Anderson, *Out of the Depths*, p. 101.

16. For the view that the 'I' of the Psalms in a number of cases was the king see especially Johnson, *the Cultic Prophet and Israel's Psalmody*; Eaton, *Kingship and the Psalms*; Croft, *The Identity of the Individual in the Psalms*.

17. Johnson, *The One and the Many in the Israelite Conception of God*, pp. 7ff.

18. Wolff, *Anthropology of the Old Testament*, pp. 219f.

19. See e.g. Kraus, *Psalms*, Vol. I, p. 342 on Ps. 28:8: '[A]n individual constantly participates in a larger reality of salvation, one that encompasses and supports his individual fate.'

Bibliography

Commentaries on the Psalms

Anderson, A. A., *Psalms*, 2 Vols. New Century Bible, London, Marshall, Morgan and Scott, 1972.

Augustine, *Expositions on The Book of Psalms*, 6 Vols. Library of the Fathers, Oxford, J. H. Parker, 1847–57.

Braude, W. G., *The Midrash on the Psalms*, 2 Vols. New Haven, Yale University Press, 1959.

Briggs, C. A., and E. G., *A Critical and Exegetical Commentary on the Book of Psalms*, 2 Vols. ICC, Edinburgh, T & T Clark, 1906.

Buttenweiser, M., *The Psalms*, Library of Biblical Studies, New York, Ktav Publishing House, 1969.

Davidson, R., *The Vitality of Worship: A Commentary on the Book of Psalms*, Grand Rapids, Michigan, Eerdmans, 1998.

Delitzsch, F., *Biblical Commentary on the Psalms*, translated by F. Bolton. 3 Vols. London, Hodder and Stoughton, 1887.

Eaton. J. H., *Psalms*, Torch Bible Commentaries, London, SCM Press, 1967.

Kirkpatrick, A. F., *The Book of Psalms*, Cambridge Bible, Cambridge, Cambridge University Press, 1902.

Kraus, H-J., *Psalms*, 2 Vols. Translated by H. C. Oswald. Minneapolis, Augsburg, 1993.

Oesterley, W. O. E., *The Psalms*, London, SPCK, 1962.

Schaefer, K., *Psalms*, Berit Olam, Studies in Hebrew Narrative and Poetry, Collegeville MN, The Liturgical Press, 2001.

Tehillim: The Book of Psalms: A New Translation with a Commentary Anthologized from Talmudic, Midrashic and Rabbinic Sources, Artscroll Tanakh Series, 2 Vols. New York, Mesorah Publications, 1985.

Weiser, A., *The Psalms: A Commentary*. Translated by H. Hartwell. Old Testament Library, London, SCM Press, 1962.

Other Works

Albright, W. F., *The Archaeology of Palestine*, Harmondsworth, Penguin, 1949.

Alter, R., *The Art of Biblical Poetry*, Edinburgh, T & T Clark, 1985.

Anderson, B. W., with Bishop, S., *Out of the Depths: The Psalms Speak for Us Today*. 3rd Edition, Louisville, Westminster John Knox Press, 2000

—— *Contours of Old Testament Theology*, Minneapolis, Fortress Press, 1999.

Balentine, S. E., *The Hidden God: The Hiding of the Face of God in the Old Testament*, Oxford, Oxford University Press, 1983.

Barr, J., *The Concept of Biblical Theology: An Old Testament Perspective*, London, SCM Press, 1999.

—— *The Semantics of Biblical Language*, London, SCM Press, 1983.

Barton, J., *Reading the Old Testament: Method in Biblical Study*, London, Darton, Longman & Todd, 2nd Edition, 1996.

Birkeland, H., *The Evildoers in the Book of Psalms*, Oslo, 1955.

Botterweck, G. & Ringgren, H. (eds), *Theological Dictionary of the Old Testament*, Grand Rapids MI, Eerdmans, 1974.

Brock, S., *The Luminous Eye: The Spiritual World Vision of Saint Ephrem the Syrian*, Kalamazoo MI, Cistercian Publications, 1992.

——*The Syriac Fathers on Prayer and the Spiritual Life*, Kalamazoo, Cistercian Publications, 1987.

Brown, D., *Tradition and Imagination: Revelation and Change*, Oxford, Oxford University Press, 1999.

——*Discipleship and Imagination: Christian Tradition and Truth*, Oxford, Oxford University Press, 2000.

Brown, F., Driver, S. R., and Briggs, C. A., *A Hebrew and English Lexicon of the Old Testament*, Oxford, Clarendon Press, 1906.

Brown, S. J., *Image and Truth: Studies in the Imagery of the Bible*, Rome, Catholic Book Agency, 1955.

Broyles, C. C., *The Conflict of Faith and Experience in the Psalms*, Sheffield, JSOT Press, 1989.

Brueggemann, W., *Israel's Praise: Doxology Against Idolatry and Ideology*, Philadelphia, Fortress Press, 1988.

——*Theology of the Old Testament*, Minneapolis, Fortress Press, 1997.

Buber, M., *I and Thou*, A new translation with a prologue and notes by Walter Kaufmann, Edinburgh, T & T Clark, 1970.

Caird, G.B., *The Language and Imagery of the Bible*, London, Duckworth, 1980.

Childs, B. S., *Myth and Reality in the Old Testament*, London, SCM Press, 1960.

Coggins, R. J. and Houlden, J. L. (eds), *A Dictionary of Biblical Interpretation*, London, SCM Press, 1990.

Croft, S. J. L., *The Identity of the Individual in the Psalms*, Sheffield, JSOT Press, 1987.

Cross, F. M., *Canaanite Myth and Hebrew Epic*, Cambridge MA, Harvard University Press, 1973.

Davis, E. F., 'Exploding the Limits: Form and Function in Psalm 22', in Clines D. J. A., (ed.) *The Poetical Books: A Sheffield Reader*, Sheffield, Sheffield Academic Press, 1997.

Day, J., *God's Conflict with the Dragon of the Sea*, Cambridge, Cambridge University Press, 1985.

——*Psalms*, Old Testament Guides, Sheffield, Sheffield Academic Press, 1992.

——*Yahweh and the Gods and Goddesses of Canaan*, Sheffield, Sheffield Academic Press, 2000.

Eaton, J. H., *Kingship and the Psalms*, London, SCM Press, 1976.

Eichrodt, W., *Theology of the Old Testament*, 2 Vols. London, SCM Press, 1961 and 1967.

Gibson, J. C. L., *Imagery and Language in the Old Testament*, London, SPCK, 1998.

Gillingham, S., *The Poems and Psalms of the Hebrew Bible*, Oxford, Oxford University Press, 1994.

Gouldner, M. D., *The Psalms of the Sons of Korah*, Sheffeld, JSOT Press, 1982.

Grant, R. M. with Tracy, D., *A Short History of the Interpretation of the Bible*, London, SCM Press, 1984.

Gray, J., *The Biblical Doctrine of the Reign of God*, Edinburgh, T & T Clark, 1979.

Hooke, S. H. (ed.), *Myth and Ritual*, Oxford, Oxford University Press, 1933.

Hastings, J. (ed.), *A Dictionary of the Bible*, 5 Vols., Edinburgh, T & T Clark, 1898.

Jacobi, J., *Complex, Archetype, Symbol in the Psychology of C. G. Jung*, Princeton, Princeton University Press, 1959.

Johnson, A., *The Cultic Prophet and Israel's Psalmody*, Cardiff, University of Wales Press, 1979.

——*The One and the Many in the Israelite Conception of God*, Cardiff, University of Wales Press, 1961.

Keel, O., *The Symbolism of the Biblical World*, London, SPCK, 1978.

Kraus, H-J., *Theology of the Psalms*, Minneapolis, Fortress Press, 1992.

Kugel, J., *The Idea of Biblical Poetry*, Baltimore, John Hopkins University Press, 1981.

Levenson, J. D., *Creation and the Persistence of Evil: The Jewish Drama of Divine Omnipotence*, Princeton, Princeton University Press, 1988.

Levine, H. J., *Sing unto God a New Song: A Contemporary Reading of the Psalms*, Bloomington, Indiana University Press, 1995.

Lewis, C. D., *The Poetic Image*, London, Jonathan Cape, 1947.

Lindström, F., *Suffering and Sin: Interpretations of Illness in the Individual Complaint Psalms*, Stockholm, Almqvist & Wiksell, 1994.

Luckman, H. A. and Kulzer, L. (eds), *Purity of Heart in Early Ascetic and Monastic Literature*, Collegeville, The Liturgical Press, 1999.

Luther, M., *Works, Vol. 14, Selected Psalms III*, Edited by J. Pelican, St Louis, Concordia Publishing House, 1958.

Macmurray, J., *Persons in Relation*, London, Faber and Faber, 1961.

Magonet, J., *A Rabbi Reads the Psalms*, London, SCM Press, 1994.

May, H. G., 'Some Cosmic Connotations of *Mayim Rabbîm*, "Many Waters"', *JBL*, LXXIV (1955) 9–21.

Miller, P. D., *Interpreting the Psalms*, Philadelphia, Fortress Press, 1986.

——*Israelite Religion and Biblical Theology*, Sheffield, Sheffield Academic Press, 2000.

Mowinckel, S., *The Psalms in Israel's Worship*, Sheffield, JSOT Press, 1992.

Murray, R., *The Cosmic Covenant*, London, Sheed and Ward, 1992.

Nasuti, H. P., *Defining the Sacred Songs*, Sheffield, Sheffield Academic Press, 1999.

Pfeiffer, R. H., *Introduction to the Old Testament*, London, A & C Black, 1952.

Pritchard, J. B. (ed.), *Ancient Near Eastern Texts Relating to the Old Testament*, Princeton, Princeton University Press, 1954.

Richardson, A. (ed), *A Theological Word Book of the Bible*, London, SCM Press, 1950.

Ricoeur, P., *The Symbolism of Evil*, New York, Harper and Row, 1967.

Rogerson, J. W., *Myth in Old Testament Interpretation*, Berlin, Walter de Gruyter, 1974.

Ryken, L. *et al.* (eds), *Dictionary of Biblical Imagery*, Leicester, Inter-Varsity Press, 1998.

Ryrie, A. C., *Silent Waiting: The Biblical Roots of Contemplative Spirituality*, Norwich, Canterbury Press, 1999.

Sacchi, P., *The History of the Second Temple Period*, Sheffield, Sheffield Academic Press, 2000.

Samuels, A. *et al.* (eds), *A Critical Dictionary of Jungian Analysis*, New York, RKP, 1986.

Sandford, J. A., *Evil, the Shadow Side of Reality*, New York, Crossroad, 1981.

Schökel, L. A., *A Manual of Hebrew Poetics*, Rome, Editrice Pontificio Istituto Biblico, 1988.

Simon, Uriel, *Four Approaches to the Book of Psalms: From Saadiah Gaon to Abraham ibn Ezra*, Albany, State University of New York Press, 1991.

Tanakh, The Holy Scriptures, Philadelphia, Jewish Publication Society, 1985.

Terrien, S., *The Elusive Presence*, San Fransisco, Harper and Row, 1978.

Tournay, R. J., *Seeing and Hearing with the Psalms*, Sheffield, JSOT Press, 1991.

von Rad, G., *Genesis: A Commentary*, Old Testament Library, London, SCM Press, rev. edn. 1972.

——*Old Testament Theology*, 2 Vols, London, SCM Press, 1975.

Wakeman, M. K., *God's Battle with the Monster: A Study in Biblical Imagery*, Leiden, E. J. Brill, 1973.

Ward, B. (ed.), *The Sayings of the Desert Fathers*, London, Mowbray, 1975.

Watson, G. E. W., *Classical Hebrew Poetry*, Sheffield, Sheffield Academic Press, 1984.

Westermann, C., *Praise and Lament in the Psalms*, Edinburgh, T & T Clark, 1981.

Wolff, H. W., *Anthropology of the Old Testament*, London, SCM Press, 1974.

Young, F., *The Art of Performance*, London, Darton, Longman & Todd, 1990.

Index of Biblical References